THE
CRYSTAL SYSTEM

WRITTEN BY

PATRICIA PITT

THE CRYSTAL SYSTEM
PATRICIA PITT

Published by in 2015 by
Tipster Publishing, Staffordshire.

A CIP Catalogue of this book is available
from the British Library

ISBN: 978-0-9934784-0-6 Paperback

Illustrated by Patricia Pitt

Designed and typeset
by Chandler Book Design
www.chandlerbookdesign.co.uk

Printed in Great Britain by
TJ International, Padstow, Cornwall

CONTENTS

Acknowledgements   vii

About The Author   ix

About the System   xi

Introduction   1
    Another Training System – Why?   2
    Self-Help   4

1. The Crystal System 5 D's   9
    Drive   9
    Dream   10
    Define   10
    Discover   10
    Do   11
    The Discipline Of Dressage   12
    Being Disciplined in Dressage   12

2. DRIVE – I want to Ride Well   13

3. DREAM - Turn your Dream into a goal   25
    Step 1: Setting Goals for the Big Picture   27
    Step 2: Trimming Down, Setting   30
    Smaller Goals
    Milestones   31
    SMART Goals   32
    Staying On Course   35
    Goal Setting Examples   36
    My Personal Goals   38

4. DEFINE – Are you FIT?   43
    Stamina   44
    Strength   45
    Agility   46
    Flexibility   46
    Balance   47
    Co-ordination   47
    Reaction Time   49
    General Health   49

5. DEFINE – Are you FIT FOR PURPOSE?   51

6. DISCOVER – Clarity in your Thinking   55

7. DISCOVER - The Beauty in your Body   63
    Head and Neck   65
    Arms and Shoulders   67
    Hands and Wrists   69
    Elbows   72
    Breathing   73
    Pelvis and Hips   76
      Independence   76
      Open Your Hips   77
      Align The Hips   77
      Following   78
      The Psoas Muscles   78
    Seat Bones And Neutral Spine   81
    Buttocks   83
    Upper Thigh   84

Knees 85

Calf and Ankles 86

Feet 87

A note about asymmetry … 88

8. DO – The Simple Things Matter 93

Feeling The Basics 96

9. DO – Your Horse's Way of Going 101

Forward 101

Are You Blocking With Your Seat? 103

Are You Blocking With Your Leg? 104

Are You Blocking With The Hand? 104

Rhythm and Relaxation 104

Tempo 107

Straightness 109

10. DO – Influencing Your Horse 113

Staying In Balance 115

A Useful Contact 117

Why Do You Ride Your Horse 'On The Bit'? 118

How Do I Know I Have A Connection? 119

Where Do I Start? 120

Testing The Connection – Stretchy Circle 122

Testing The Connection – Give And Re-take 122

A Word Of Caution 123

Maintaining The Outline 123

Inside Leg To Outside Hand 124

Developing The Half Halt 125

Working in a Long and Low Frame 128

The Power of Transitions 130

The Upward Transition 132

The Canter Depart 132

The Downward Transition 133

Developing Variation in the Strides 135

Slowing the Canter 136

Use of the Canter to Walk Transition 141

Shapes and Accuracy 142

Walk Your Way to Success 142

Halt, Immobility, Salute 143

11. DO - Suppling your Horse 145

Bending And Turning 146

Figure of Eight 147

The Tear Drop Turn 148

Shoulder-Fore / Shoulder-In 149

Between Shoulder-Fore and Quarters-In 151

Working In A Long and Low Frame 152

The Warm Up 152

12. DO - Rider Focus Plan 157

The Rider Focus Plan 161

RIDER FOCUS PLAN Example 162

My Focus Plan 163

13. Overcoming a Crisis 167

Reframe Your Thinking 168

Emotional Intelligence 170

Crystallized and Fluid Intelligence 173

Get Excited and Go - Competition Nerves 173

Make Failure Your Friend 179

Acknowledgements

I wish to extend my personal thanks to the following people for their contributions to creation of this book:

Jay White Digital Art for taking my pencil drawings and bringing Crystal to life; Blue Chip Feeds, Shoe Secure and Kitt Equestrian for their continued support and for the consistency of their remarkable products and services.

The Crystal System Test Pilots, Amanda Crowley, Sue Clark of Motueka Dressage, N.Z. and Helen Mathie, MSc BSc (Hons) MCSP SRP ACPAT A of Aegrus Equestrian, whose contribution is immeasurable.

John Chandler of Chandler Book Design for seeing my vision and delivering it but more than that, for stepping in with help and guidance above and beyond his brief.

And of course to my Mum and Dad, Rita and Ken Sammons – "All that I am or hope to be I owe to the start my mother and father gifted me".

About The Author

Patricia Pitt is an award winning blogger from Huntington, Staffordshire, U.K. Known as The Dressage Tipster, in her blog at www.likecrystal.com she regularly shares what she has learned from her research into why becoming truly skilled in the art of dressage is so elusive to so many riders.

With burning aspirations to be able to ride well she became incredibly frustrated at her lack of progress and inability to find the keys to unlock her riding potential. Turning to her long suffering partner Mark Bentley, who was trained by the very best from the first time he sat in the saddle, she made a commitment to learn from him. By doing so, she has gained an insight into the extent of what is required; where she was going wrong and found that this resonates with many, many grassroots riders. The process has enabled her to develop and share with you a progressive system of training that will aid your progress by asking you to question everything you do. Looking at how you think about your riding; how your body works and how your horse responds to your signals.

The system walks you through a process of self-assessment and planning of your training, giving you hints and tips to take into the arena, all in plain English making very easy reading.

About the System

Many horse riding training methods and systems of training are mechanical; techniques which the trainer will try to instil in a pupil.

To ride well you need 'feel', which is not only difficult to teach, it's difficult for a trainer to explain and difficult for a rider to grasp. It helps if you can develop sensitivity and tact; build your body so that it can work with the horse's movement; understand the affects you are having on your horse and understand what is at the heart of everything you do.

The Crystal System is a self-help system, which unravels the mysteries surrounding that elusive ability to ride skilfully.

You will, without doubt, have several Eureka moments, when you recognise that your heroic efforts have been hindering you. You do not need to work physically hard. The work comes from activating your brain and the realisation that, if only someone had offered you a way to plan your training, broken down the process, rider to rider and kept it simple, all your hard work would have reaped the rewards you dream of.

The Crystal System will give you the confidence to select the very best from your experiences and develop your own understanding of how to train your horse. Through questioning and exploration of what you do, the Crystal System will allow you to identify, develop and mould your own system of training as your learning and experience grows. This approach enables you to discover for yourself what it means to be able to 'ride well'.

Introduction

Dressage is one of the fastest growing equestrian sports in Great Britain. Often thought of as an elitist sport, participation at all levels, from grassroots up to Grand Prix, has risen steeply in recent times.

Historically, International Dressage has been dominated by Germany and the Netherlands with Sweden, Austria, Finland, Spain, USA and Great Britain having a presence and individual success to some extent but never presenting a real challenge to the ever victorious German and Dutch teams.

Having made it to seventh place in the 2008 Olympics, Team GB tinkered around the edges of success but was never a threat to the dominating Dressage nations and certainly never in contention for medals. All that changed, when in 2009 the British Team gained Silver in the European Championships. 2010 bought Silver in the World Equestrian Games. Britain won Gold at the Europeans in 2011 and of course nailed its first ever Olympic Gold Medal in Dressage in 2012.

Fast forward to 2014 and Charlotte Dujardin with her superhorse, Valegro are on top of the world having secured the 2014 Reem Acra World Championship, giving this British combination every accolade available to a top level dressage rider and what's more for the first time in history she has secured all these titles at the same time.

World No. 1 Ranking	European Individual and Team Gold	Olympic Individual and Team Gold	World Championship	World Records in Grand Prix, Grand Prix Special and Freestyle

This is a truly outstanding achievement. Charlotte, her team-mate, trainer and mentor Carl Hester, who is currently considered one of the greatest Dressage equestrians in history and her contemporary Laura Tomlinson, who has also held the World No. 1 Ranking and stood alongside Charlotte and Carl on the Olympic podium have catapulted British Dressage into previously unmarked territory for the British Team. Never before has such a feat been achieved, thus demonstrating the effect of good training and true dedication. Not only have Charlotte and Valegro conquered the world, but Charlotte and Carl are lauded as having produced the ultimate, happy athlete.

Charlotte's story is well known. She arrived at Carl's yard as a groom and 18 months after riding her first ever Grand Prix is the World's No. 1 Dressage Rider.

Your dreams may be somewhat smaller, but nonetheless challenging, as are mine. Bourne out of awful frustration at a lack of progression The Crystal System has been developed as a pathway through the fog, a clear and transparent method, in plain English; a systematic and easy to apply, staged program that will help you to think for yourself and train your horse for yourself. A self-help manual for dressage riders, giving you the tools you need to guide you through the issues; come up with the solutions and achieve the improvement; absolute control for you and your horse.

ANOTHER TRAINING SYSTEM – WHY?

I don't really know where the spark came from. It was spring, my favourite season and after a very, very long winter I should have felt good. I didn't. I'd been working with my horse for a few weeks and having the same old problems, but this day a spark inside me came to life. I could not go on getting nowhere. I needed something else, but what? That day, my journey started.

My partner, Mark Bentley, on the other hand had always been a natural rider, you know the type of rider who can apply himself, with determination and discipline and 'it' happens, and not just happens but with great subtlety and finesse.

When he started riding dressage he walked straight up to a former National Champion at the Winter National Championships and asked him if he could go to him for training. He had a 4 year old, just backed Lusitano mare and could barely keep his feet in the stirrups, let alone ride a circle. That was the start for Mark and with his usual level of fortitude and commitment he stated "I will ride Medium level competition in a year". And he did. He trained that horse himself all the way up to Grand Prix level. Dressage seems so easy for him.

I, on the other hand, made gargantuan physical efforts to sit correctly, apply the right technique, research and acquire as much knowledge as I could. Technically I knew a great deal, but simply could not find the recipe to make 'it' happen. I found myself horribly frustrated at my lack of progress, often giving up at the first, sometimes the second hurdle and always marking time. It became apparent to me that my riding instructors (of which there have been many) had not helped but hindered my progression. Yes, I could ride but I had no 'feel', I was very mechanical in my thinking and in the delivery of my aids, was unable to be elegant. I could not see a way of reaching my dream of being a proficient rider. All this is ok, I suppose. What isn't ok is the way it made me feel about myself; essentially an epic fail. Something was missing and I knew it. I felt there must be other riders who were having similar experiences. I could see in my immediate locality, a number of fellow equestrians who appeared to have the same issue, lack of real progression. Competitions above the level of Novice are very poorly attended in my area. My contemporaries however, appeared not to be quite so frustrated by it as I was. I guess 'you don't know, what you don't know' if that makes any sense, but now I knew and I had to do something different.

I decided there and then that I would find out why my dream was so elusive. I purchased every book on every method of training that was available, from the classical masters to the latest science. That was a really interesting time for me, each of them had something to offer, but none of them inspired me to follow their method wholeheartedly. None of them, I felt, got to the very heart of the matter. Remember, that I was already fairly knowledgeable, in theory, which in my view many grass roots riders are, finding that mysterious ingredient that would stimulate me sufficiently to say to me "yes, that's how it should be done" just was not in any of those books.

I extracted from Mark his philosophy and made a commitment to learn from him. I would make amends and share my findings with everyone. It was having this 'light bulb moment' or 'epiphany' which galvanised me to develop The Crystal System. I found myself with a yearning to help others like myself but was halted by doubts of whether anyone would want to listen to me or that once I started I wouldn't have enough to say. That's funny! I soon discovered that the ideas I now have an insight into resonate with many, many riders and I have already seriously helped them in their struggle. Believe me when I tell you, I've got plenty to say.

I managed to convince myself that when someone is so passionate about something, they must know something worth sharing, right? I am, by no means, an expert; I just want to share what I know. And hey, I really don't profess to be 'all knowing', Dressage is a life-long journey of discovery and I will share with you my views based on my experiences. So why would you listen to me? Because we share this passion, because I am following my heart and that's what you want and because I may just be able to help you. That's all.

SELF-HELP

When we think of self-help it can sometimes have negative connotations. Conjuring up images of a 'Billy-No-Mates' type character, having to do things alone, having to become independent and tough but actually if you break the term down to 'self' and 'help', the 'self' part just means working on one's own problems. Of course, they are going to be slightly unique and different from others, you and your horse are two living beings, how could your difficulties exactly replicate those of your contemporaries? However, the basic essential means of working doesn't have to be that much different. It's a principle, and you can apply the principle to your unique set of circumstances whilst working with others and still get a friendly, supportive, group thing going on, with you controlling the way in which you do it.

'Self' doesn't mean working alone and therefore, by definition, lonely. It actually means 'the use of one's own efforts and resources to achieve things without relying on others'. I'm sure you want that. I know I did.

The 'help' element of the term refers to seeking help that can be implemented by you. To invest in change by considering and working on the many alternatives that may address your particular set of problems, hopefully with significant results. Most dressage enthusiasts know or at least have heard of the German Scales of Training - Rhythm, Suppleness, Contact, Impulsion, Straightness and Collection. When riding dressage it can be helpful to think of your passage to becoming an effective rider in the same way, in stages that are building blocks, similar to the training scale. Because without addressing each element of the rider's training scale, in the correct order, you will be pushing yourself before you are ready, rather like trying to ask a young horse that is just finding his rhythm, to perform Piaffe. Training you to train horses, means approaching the challenge in the way you would train a horse. Starting with the basics; understanding where you are in the process and using building blocks to build strong and solid foundations.

Using The Crystal System will teach you that most elusive of skills which is so obviously missing from most training methods. I have to use a number of words because no one word will suffice – skill, flair, grace, elegance, poise, assurance, refinement, subtlety, tact – FEEL! Many horse training methods and systems of training are mechanical; techniques which the trainer will try to instil in a pupil. Feel is not only difficult to teach, it's difficult for the trainer to explain and difficult for the rider to grasp. The Crystal System is a powerful, thought provoking, formula which, if followed and applied correctly, can aid progress towards you and your horse being the dressage divas that you so aspire to be. With the help of Crystal, the cartoon character inspired by Mark's very own Lusitano mare, Sintra, I hope to lighten your spirits and inject a little fun along the way.

$$R^2 + F + H^2 = IMPULSION$$

Dressage is perceived as all very difficult

During my research I found that dressage is perceived as incredibly complicated and difficult. The Crystal System attempts to unravel the mysteries surrounding that indefinable ability to ride skilfully. It breaks down the jargon and the flowery speak, explains in plain English exactly what is required.

You will, without doubt, have several 'eureka moments', when you realise your heroic efforts have been hindering you and if only someone had broken it down, rider to rider, instead of fashioning some complicated 'mumbo-jumbo' you would have got there. If you are an experienced rider it will help you restructure your training, rethink your approach, look at things a little differently. This will enable you to discover for yourself what it means to be able to 'ride well'.

Once you have sorted out any body parts that do not function properly, you do not need to work physically hard, you need to work by activating your brain. The Crystal System will give you the confidence to select the very best from your experiences and develop your own understanding of how to train your horse(s) and your horse's individual needs. It will show you how to cultivate sensitivity and tact, build your body and mind so that they can work in unity with your horse and help you to foster the ability to 'weigh up' your horse's state of mind. There will always be a place for technique, but only as a tool, it is not the end goal. Let's get you on track with your riding, feeling energised and focussed, able to set clear goals and feel able to achieve them. This is what grass roots riding is all about, attainable by anyone with a desire to succeed and putting into place the essentials to go on to advanced levels.

Attitudes I have encountered range from "isn't riding supposed to be fun?" and "it's your hobby, you shouldn't feel discomfort" to "why so frustrated?" All I can say is that these opinions must originate in the myth that you can master the art of dressage without too much effort. Unfortunately, I have discovered that mastering a skill cannot be accomplished with complacency and superficial thrill seeking. It is only with serious study for a long period, sometimes years and genuine, guided effort which encompasses the mind, body and heart can one master a skill. This is something many riders don't realise or acknowledge. This is the essence of what you must embrace and enjoy.

You will, without doubt, have several eureka moments

Not everyone will agree with the Crystal System; not everyone will want to do it this way; not everyone will have what it takes; not everyone will see the results that I saw; but some will and that's why I created The Crystal System. I get asked all the time "do you have to have a special horse?" The answer is no, well, yes and no. No, because every horse is capable of dressage at some level. It is up to you to get the best out of you both as a team. Yes, because your horse is your partner, you have a journey to travel together; you should recognise that as 'special'.

Throughout the book I will give you a myriad of information. Whilst writing this book I had a very enthusiastic test pilot working through the system, chapter by chapter. She got so excited in the early days that it simply wasn't possible to make all the changes she needed to make in one go, so when she tried, she found that she could not improve anything. Becoming disillusioned and throwing her arms up in the air, saying 'I knew it wouldn't work!' She was the victim of reading half a book; I tell you this now as a warning. In time, with the benefit of the last couple of chapters, she took a step back and made a plan which cleared the path for her. It would be awesome if you get really excited and want to dash off and try everything like my test pilot but your horse won't appreciate it and ultimately neither will you. You need to prioritise and ensure that you don't do too much too soon.

The Crystal System works towards one 'big picture', helping you to understand that you are now an eternal student. The more you learn the more you will realise that you do not know. You will be on this journey for your whole life and each achievement, however, large or small will build towards the ultimate training goal – being 'as one' with your horse.

Build towards your ultimate training goal … being 'as one' with your horse

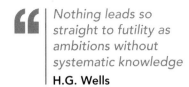

Nothing leads so straight to futility as ambitions without systematic knowledge

H.G. Wells

The Crystal System 5 D's

Through questioning and exploration of why and how you ride The Crystal System will allow you to identify, develop and mould your own system of training as your learning and experience grows.

DRIVE

The first stage of the system looks at the driving force behind what makes you want to do this. Knowing the reason you want to ride well is a vigorous motivator. It's not enough to just want it, you really do need to determine why. Really good riders establish a way of thinking which for them creates incentives to take on the necessary actions and choices that leave them no other path to follow than the one which leads directly to their training success. You too can begin to piece together a plan that will keep your enthusiasm; a plan that will stimulate you to achieve; a plan that will be the driving force behind everything you do both in the saddle and out of it.

The Crystal System 5 D's

The hope is, as you progress through the book, you will become hungry for knowledge, hungry to put that knowledge into practice and enjoy every minute of the challenges you face, more and more, just as I did.

Often riders are set adrift, working hard but not getting anywhere worthwhile.

DREAM

The second stage helps you to determine what you want from this process. Having a clear and concise set of goals that you can refer to and adjust throughout your journey will keep your dream alive and help you get there.

By knowing precisely what you want to achieve, you know where you have to concentrate your efforts. Often riders feel like they are set adrift, working hard but not really getting anywhere worthwhile. They may be doing what the trainer says but not really 'owning' what is being advised and often not really understanding why or indeed, how to do these things properly. Understanding what your dream actually might look like, that's really empowering.

DEFINE

Dressage is about creating happy athletes. That's you and your horse. The third stage of this program helps you to define where you are currently in terms of your physical fitness and ability to be an athlete.

This fairly short section will walk you through what you need to take account of to be an athlete; helping you think about every aspect of rider fitness.

DISCOVER

Next, the discovery phase comes in two parts: Clarity in Your Thinking and The Beauty in Your Body. The Crystal System will encourage you in the way you think about your training; establish how you are going to go about it and put yourself into the right mind-set to make the most of your training sessions.

Taking you through a top to toe analysis of you as a rider and asking you to look at your body and its capabilities; identifying difficulties you might have in manoeuvring yourself into that often elusive, effective position on your horse.

Exercises and Crystal's Tips will help you to discover for yourself a number of small yet, highly effective ways of positioning yourself to achieve the optimum seat for dressage. The hope is that you will want to go and get on your horse, practice and then come back to tick off another of those goals.

The discovery phase can be quite humbling and you will need an open mind. Any unwillingness to consider new ideas is often the result of the brain's natural dislike for vagueness which is why my mission is to keep everything as clear and simple as possible. I sometimes get my non-horsey friends to read my blog articles and if they require too much explanation, I go back and look again at the wording. This process is a useful tool, go back, look again and find the heart of the problem. Be very clear and transparent. I urge you to try and not be afraid to challenge your long held beliefs; to be very honest with yourself about your achievements and how you feel; to break down what you think is right and not so right; to believe in yourself and find your way.

DO

The final stage of the Crystal System will give you more exercises, hints and tips to help you on your way to enjoying the skills you have to train your horse for yourself. Everything a young or novice horse and rider need to enable a self-check that the whole thing is right before you progress up the training ladder. For those already competing above this level it will serve as a useful checking mechanism to consolidate the work you have already undertaken, ensuring your future success and ability to make further progress more easily.

The 'Do' phase outlines only what I believe are the essential exercises and principles that you need to master. Clearly you could not put into one book everything that is needed, but if you master this set of exercises and guidelines they will serve you well in every future endeavour. Finally the 'Do' phase will facilitate pulling together all that you have gleaned from previous chapters and help you to make a plan to focus on the priorities you identify.

THE DISCIPLINE OF DRESSAGE

Throughout the entire Crystal System process you will need to embrace another 'D' word – Discipline. Discipline is the bridge between your goals and accomplishment of them; the thread that holds the pieces of the training together; the silk that forms your spider's web.

In its original sense, discipline is systematic instruction intended to train a person, sometimes literally called a discipline, an art form, a craft, a trade or activity, or to follow a particular code of conduct or order and so we talk about the discipline of dressage or the Art of Dressage. Often, the phrase 'to discipline' carries a negative connotation. This is because enforcement of order, that is, ensuring instructions are carried out, is often regulated through punishment. In this sense discipline plays no part in dressage.

BEING DISCIPLINED IN DRESSAGE

The second level use of the word discipline relates to a course of actions leading to certain goals or ideals. A disciplined person is one that has established a goal and is willing to achieve that goal no matter what occurs and it is discipline that enables the assertion of willpower over more base desires, usually synonymous with self-control. Self-discipline is to some extent a substitute for motivation, when you do what needs to be done and do that even when you don't feel like doing it, that's when you have a healthy level of self-control.

Crystal Says

So, let's find your motivation.

I believe that anything in life that is worth having is worth working for. Yes, we do dressage because we enjoy it, but it is 'serious fun' not 'jolly-holiday' type fun. We need a disciplined approach in order to cut our way through the glut of information and concentrate on what is significant to us at that moment in time. We need discipline to stay focussed and we need discipline to follow the plans we lay down, after all the pain of self-discipline will never be as great as the pain of regret.

*The secret to getting
ahead is getting started*
Mark Twain

DRIVE – I want to Ride Well

At the start of my journey I had a vague idea I wanted to ride well. I wasn't really sure what that meant and certainly wasn't prepared for how strong this 'want' would become.

Wanting to learn is an important element of attaining success. I like the word 'wanting', it is a powerful, basic human drive. 'Motivation', although it might mean the same thing, is a word to dispassionately describe 'wanting'.

As I progressed through my training, I become hungry for knowledge about how my body worked, hungry to put that knowledge into practice, shape my position and enjoy the challenges I faced. I am hoping you will feel this way too. It's pretty addictive. When you really want something, you usually get it sooner or later. I have discovered the only way to see real improvement is to re-examine and question everything we do; keep the good things and reject the bad things. I found this because to this day, no matter what training issues I encounter, the solution is always somewhere in the basics and more often than not, in the way I ride.

The process of finding my own rider faults, after many years of riding, took a somewhat penetrating examination of my motives, convictions, attitudes, an in depth analysis of myself in an effort to determine my true feelings, capabilities and beliefs. This all began with the admission that I was not nearly as good as I thought I was. I questioned everything I had accomplished, everything I thought I knew. The anguish that is caused by this process, and the honesty which is vital for it, is immense.

Take a long and honest look at yourself and your current skill levels.

Motivation is the force that initiates, guides and maintains your behaviour. We all have basic human needs, some of which are pretty simple - food, sleep, shelter, water. If these are not met we suffer emotionally, no doubt about that, but then I don't suppose for one moment anyone who has purchased a self-help book for dressage riders does not have the basic need for food and water met.

We also have emotional needs. To be emotionally healthy we need to feel safe, regularly give and receive quality attention, be able to feel in control of our lives, feel part of a community, enjoy friendship, fun, love and intimacy. We need to feel recognised and competent. Knowing and understanding this is the first step to creating focus in your training that is not affected by and actually goes beyond your emotions.

ASK YOURSELF:

Is there an incentive? Is your motivation some sort of external reward? Can you get sponsorship perhaps?

What is driving you? Is there a tension that needs addressing? Is riding a release?

Is it the excitement of the riding that motivates you? The thrill of the competition?

Maybe it is a humanistic motivation. With your basic hierarchy of needs met (food, water, sleep and warmth, safety and security) we move onto the need or desire for you to fulfil your own individual potential. Are you driven by your desire to gain a skill?

Do you do it for love, companionship or friendship?

Maybe it's all about your confidence and self-worth. Perhaps you feel like you're a fraud, an imposter, or simply not good enough? The dressage fraternity can do that to you.

I was surprised to learn that the vast majority of successful people feel like impostors from time to time; it's actually a positive sign. Feelings of faking it are usually associated with intelligence, diligence and, paradoxically, competence. Slackers, blusterers and the genuinely incompetent tend not to stress about feeling like fakers.

Give yourself some time to think about your needs and how your life, not just the equine area of your life, is meeting them. Write down your thoughts. If there are any deficiencies, work out activities that are likely to help you fulfil them. Whilst you are starting this process, as far as your riding is concerned go back to your early riding days; feel the freedom that sitting on a horse gave you; keep sight of the pleasure of riding a horse; take a moment to feel the privilege.

Feeling like a fraud, an imposter, or simply not good enough?

Bruce Lee is considered the martial arts master. It is an unlikely comparison but for me martial arts and dressage have a great deal in common. A great deal of what we do is about the way we think, the approach we take and the patience, dedication and discipline required to achieve real success. Bruce Lee's philosophy is worth studying if you really want to succeed, not just at riding but at anything that is worthwhile in life.

So much of what we read and what we are taught in dressage is difficult to understand, surrounded by a complicated and bespoke language that in itself is hard to grasp. The Crystal System endeavours to deliver its teachings in a more simplistic, easily understandable way. I have gathered a collection of Bruce Lee quotes which in the context of dressage are thought provoking and inspiring and may help you find your motivation.

***"I'm not in this world to live up to your expectations
and you're not in this world to live up to mine"***

When we move onto the goal setting stage of the program you will discover that they should always be personal. Dressage is about training and continual improvement. When you compete it is not against others but against yourself and you always aim to improve on last time. Don't be overly concerned about how others are progressing.

***"Always be yourself, express yourself, have faith in yourself, do not
go out and look for a successful personality and duplicate it"***

Developing a training method that is right for you is absolutely the only way forward. You may aspire to be able to ride like someone else, but it is the combination of you and your horse that is utterly unique. Religiously trying to replicate what your trainer does and says will not help you to train your horse. Perhaps when you are learning the basics or are floundering to find the right approach, it is good to concentrate on one method but ultimately the aim is for you to take control of your own destiny. There are many paths that lead to the same destination. Only you can work out the best route for you and your horse.

***"Absorb what is useful, discard what is not, add
what is uniquely your own"***

The most empowering aspect of this whole process to date has been that of discovering what was and wasn't working for me. Gathering knowledge, making my own mind up about what's right for me and my horse, experimenting and adding my own touches, developing my own unique system that works for me.

I loved thinking it through, working it out and developing my way of doing things. I even loved it when I found my techniques didn't work. You must not be afraid to make mistakes. You must not be afraid to follow your heart. You must not be afraid to make a u-turn or change direction. It is about your personal growth and you will not get it right every step of the way, guaranteed.

"Obey the principles without being bound by them"

How many of you have regular lessons where you're directed to 'do this' or 'do that' and you blindly follow the instruction, never really knowing why or what the true effect is. The basic principles of dressage are all the same, it's about how they are applied that makes them uniquely yours. There are many rules associated with dressage riding. How you should sit, how you should look and how you should progress. Play it all by the book and you will never be a success, because you will never develop that ever elusive element of 'feel' that is so important. Be flexible in your approach, bend the rules.

"Knowing is not enough, we must apply. Willing is not enough, we must do"

Having an in depth knowledge of anything is great isn't it? I did. I could so easily impress others with my ability to pin point what was going wrong with a rider, I could even give help and advice about how to put it right. But actually applying this knowledge to my own riding in a structured way that started with the basics and built up? Nah, couldn't do it. I had to find a way of organising the knowledge in such a way that it became easy to apply. I often think of my brain back then as a big scribbly mess. But now, having followed The Crystal System process my brain feels more like a spider's web; organised, connected, interlinked in an orderly fashion and all structured to the same central goal.

Enthusiasm, eagerness, readiness, willingness, call it what you will. Being willing to do something is admirable. But without action you are unworthy of admiration. Discipline is the assertion of willpower over more base desires; you will need this to succeed. Finding how to turn your willingness into action, that's what you need.

"As you think, so shall you become"

Dressage is very much a thinking sport. I firmly believe that the Pareto Principle (the 80/20 rule) applies here. Your training success will come from 80% thinking through the whole process and planning with the last 20% actually doing. Be positive in your thoughts, disregard all those negative thoughts that cloud your judgement and hold you back from achieving your goals. The way in which you think will determine your destination and every road en-route. Make it a positive experience for yourself.

"If you spend too much time thinking about a thing,
you'll never get it done"

Au contraire! Whilst 80% of your success will be governed by the plan you put in place and your ability to analyse and assess your performance, don't think about it for too long. You must take action otherwise you will simply never get started. Whilst, many regard procrastination as a useful way of identifying what is important to us personally, this on the basis that it is rare to procrastinate when one truly values the task at hand. Others believe that procrastination results in stress, a sense of guilt and creation of a crisis that could be avoided. As with all things, you will need to find the balance.

And my personal favourite … *"Simplicity is the key to brilliance"*

I know many very knowledgeable trainers but they are not clear about what they want let alone what they want for their pupils. Knowledge is not power. Clarity is where the empowerment comes from. The difference is in knowing what you want, day by day, one session at a time. Knowing how to put that knowledge into action effectively; having absolute clarity about where you have come from, where you are now and where you are going. Try to see through those that use flowery, self-important, 'look at how much I know' speak and find someone who will get to the root of the matter in as few words as possible. Just get clear about what you want and how to do it.

I like clarity. In fact, I am utterly obsessed with it. When I come across equestrians that fill their world with 'techie' speak I become disinterested, somehow it switches me off. After all, for me simplicity is the key to brilliance and I so want to be more than mediocre.

Ok, so you have explored why you want to ride well. Now you need to take some action and stick to it. Easier said than done when even the most driven of us can feel unmotivated at times. In fact, sometimes we get into such a slump that just thinking about making changes is tricky. Rather than feeling hopeless the thing to do is to take some small steps to change things. Baby steps in fact, to get you started down the road to positive change.

I know it can seem impossible at times. You can get confused and don't know where to start. You are not alone. But I've learned a few ways to break out of a slump. After all those years in the wilderness, my light bulb moment came when it occurred to me that I needed to do something but I wasn't quite sure what. There was so much going on in my head that it stifled me and I got to wondering why it's so hard for someone to change direction and begin to take control.

The answer is clarity. Without a clear path those baby steps I spoke of are useless, you will trot around the arena like the proverbial headless chicken. The alternative is to establish a clear path to follow and take those baby steps to a logical destination. We will explore this in Chapter Three – Turn Your Dream

Baby steps get you started down the road to positive change

Into A Goal - when we study personal goal setting. In the meantime, you have purchased this book, so my guess is that you are not quite at the low point that I was. Your thinking is perhaps not so clouded as mine. You have already taken the first positive step, so well done you.

Consider what your inspiration might be. For me inspiration comes from someone who has achieved what I want to achieve and is able to do it, Mark Bentley, my partner. Next you need to get excited. Err, yes, I hear you cry, that's obvious, but most people don't think about it much: if you want to break out of a slump, get yourself excited about what you want to do. But how can you do that when you don't feel motivated? For me, I've learned that by talking things through with Mark, by talking to fellow equestrians, reading as much as possible, visualising what it would be like to ride well, I get excited. Once I've done that, it's just a matter of carrying that energy forward and keeping it going.

Why is it so hard to change direction?

Maybe you should build anticipation, which is not easy. Don't get started start right away. Many of us will get excited and want to start today and that can often be a mistake for some people. By setting a date in the future, a week or two, or even a month, and by making that your start date, marking it on the calendar you build the anticipation and increase your focus and energy for what you are about to achieve. Most people will skip this tip but it really does work.

None of us like to look bad in front of others. We will go the extra mile to do something we've said publicly. Talk to people about what you are doing, share your thoughts on social media with your friends and hold yourself accountable. Commit to giving progress updates to everyone every week or so. You should consider getting support. It's really hard to accomplish something so very complex, alone. Find a support network, either in the real world or online, or both. Having an accountability buddy really helps. But whatever you do, don't give up. Even if you aren't feeling any motivation today, or this week, don't give up. Think of your goal as a long journey, and your slump is just a little bump in the road. You can't give up with every little bump. Stay with it for the long term, ride out the ebbs and surf on the flows, and you'll get there.

When I lose motivation, I just read a book or blog about dressage. It inspires and reinvigorates me. Reading helps motivate and focus me. You should read about your goal every day, if you can, especially when you're not feeling motivated. Think about the benefits, not the difficulties. One common problem is to think about how hard something is. Often just thinking about it makes you tired. But instead of thinking about how hard something is, think about what you will get out of it. For example, instead of thinking about how tiring it is going to the stables, tacking up and riding, focus on how good you'll feel when you're done. The fruits of your labour will help to energise you. Often when you dig deep into your 'drive reserves' and make the effort to ride you get your best results.

Squash negative thoughts and replace them with positive ones. Along similar lines, it's a good idea to start monitoring your thoughts so that you can recognise negative self-talk, something which is really going to kill your motivation. Just spend a few days becoming aware of every thought about your riding. Then, after a few days take a look at them and try to squash the negative thoughts like a bug. Reword them to a corresponding positive thought. Squash, "This is too hard" and replace it with, "I can do this". I have a friend with a challenging horse, every time she mounts she goes through the long list of negative self-talk "oh, he feels a bit wired today", "don't know if we'll get any good work today!" I just counter everything she says with a positive. "He's walking out well today", "You mounted him without any signs of stress, that's good" and it sounds corny but it does work. I even try to say my positive stuff louder so that it is the dominating thought.

Take a few minutes to jot down your initial thoughts about why you want to ride well. What is driving you to pick up this book? Why are you doing this?

DRIVE	Why are you doing this?

Success is no accident. It needs to become a habit. That seemingly magical force that has the ability to take what was, at first, difficult and, over time, through diligent practice and repetition, make it easier, effortless even. The highest form of competence is a state of natural mastery (also known as unconscious competence), where once there have been many hours of practice, it becomes harder for a person to err than to perform the task correctly. How do you achieve this state of mind? There have been many studies on the subject of sports psychology and as always the answer is through practice; you cannot stop the feelings of frustration or anxiety so you should notice them and without being judgemental about yourself, control your reactions to them. It is when in a relaxed state of concentration that the sense of effortlessness comes. Only then can you become fully immersed in the feeling of the 'here and now' because you are not reacting to the feelings or thinking of the consequences. This is called being in a 'flow' state, when you get involved in something so deeply that nothing else seems to matter and you completely lose track of time. It is a mental state of mind where a person is performing an activity and is fully immersed in a feeling of energised focus, with full involvement in the process of the activity, involving effortless concentration and enjoyment. Flow can happen when a person's skills are fully involved in overcoming a challenge that is just about manageable and so it acts as a magnet for learning new skills and increasing challenges. This little space between boredom and anxiety is the holy grail of training. Focussing wholly on the current exercise will serve to optimise cooperation and harmony between you and your horse. No matter how you are feeling, learn to say 'Hi' to those feelings but pay them no attention. Park them and continue with your training. They can sit and watch you ride well!

The real gem of information I have for you, and this is a corker, is that everyone, even you have the built-in, all powerful achievement device, a gift really. It is the ability to develop any habit necessary to help you achieve any goal or to help you realise your vision of success. We will explore this further in Chapter 12 – Do – Rider Focus Plan. For now just sit back and give some thought to your everyday habits and how they control your life. You have them don't you? We all do. Maybe you go into the coffee room at the stables on arrival and before you know it an hour of your time has gone, leaving you less time with your horse. Maybe you don't and instead miss out of the social aspect of your hobby. What you need to do is form new habits that are right for your progression and assist you achieve your dressage dream.

I have already illustrated that I wanted to ride well for many, many years. I became very frustrated and nearly gave up altogether, until I recognised that I was stuck in my ways, needed to clear my mind and be a beginner again, as if I had never ridden; accept how badly I had been taught, by people who either knew no better or didn't care enough. I needed to take a long, hard look at myself, get fit and rebuild my skills. This is the basis of The Crystal System. Believe that you will overcome any difficulties you might face, picture your success and be certain of attaining it. Be mindful that success doesn't usually happen quickly and be grateful for this. It carries with it a certain burden and you need time to prepare for the responsibility.

Don't give up easily and don't expect instant gratification. Be ready and willing to change yourself after all, it is ridiculous to expect success when you refuse to make the changes that will enable it.

Now take a little time to work out what is driving you and then we can take a look at what it is you actually want to do.

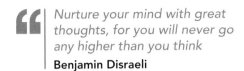

Nurture your mind with great thoughts, for you will never go any higher than you think

Benjamin Disraeli

DREAM - Turn your Dream into a goal

The human brain is a problem-solving, goal-achieving machine. Sometimes it may lack direction so knowing what you want to achieve and how you intend to achieve it will capitalise on your brain's amazing powers.

In the business world, I know people who have been the brunt of many jokes because they live by their planner. Writing down goals, having quarterly and monthly benchmarks, setting daily task lists. Task not done, not a problem, move it to the next day and make sure it gets done. These people evaluate their goals regularly and change them as the world throws in the inevitable curve balls. Goal setting is a natural part of their being, just like their eye colour.

For others setting goals is viewed as a tedious task; a necessary evil brought on by a boss. They write a few things down on paper to fulfil the requirement, knowing that it can be put aside and everyone will probably forget about it in the coming months. From my experience of goal setting in the workplace, I sat and thought about what I wanted from my riding I got to thinking …

Without goals your dreams are just wishful thinking

ASK YOURSELF:

What if goal setting really could make the difference you are looking for?

What if you actually thought through what you are aiming for with your horse?

What if you wrote it down and got a little excited about it?

I've discovered that goals are the basis for all achievement; without them you are merely wheel spinning, lacking direction. It is the process of building a road-map to your ultimate goal that is the most influential tool for helping you choose where you want to be, getting focus and crystallising your thinking. By knowing precisely what you want to achieve, you know where you have to concentrate all those considerable efforts you are putting in. Also, you can quickly spot any distractions that can, and so easily do, lead you astray.

Top-level athletes, successful business-people and achievers in all fields use the setting of goals to give long-term vision and short-term enthusiasm to their projects. It focuses the mind and helps to, not only organise, but prioritise time so that you can make the very most of it. Let's be honest, for most amateur riders there is a balancing act to be achieved in terms of time. By setting smart, clearly defined goals, you can measure and take pride in your achievements, however small. Assuming these mean something to you, you should see progress in what might previously have seemed a long and pointless grind. Goals will make you aware of your own strengths and weaknesses, so that you can begin to improve your weaknesses and turn them into strengths.

Are you sold on the idea? Are you itching to scamper off and start writing stuff down? Not yet? Here's my final pitch … goal setting will, unquestionably, build your self-confidence as you tick off your achievements and start to recognise your own abilities and competency. Goals give you a sense of past victories, of what you have accomplished and motivation to succeed in the future. It did for me and I'm convinced it will for you. Without goals your dreams are just wishful thinking, with them you have a 'call to action' after all is said and done. An idea is just a dream until you write it down, then it becomes a goal.

STEP 1: SETTING GOALS FOR THE BIG PICTURE

Let's be honest, if you don't know where you're going, you'll never get there, right? So, what if you made the decision to go down the route of setting really worthwhile goals? Think international journey as opposed to domestic flight. What would be possible if suddenly your goals were far greater than just a trip to the tack shop? I'm not talking 'set up an equine rescue centre' or 'campaign for a ban of Rollkur' (although those are absolutely worthy goals), it makes more sense to start a little closer to home and consider what for you would be the ultimate achievement with your equine friend.

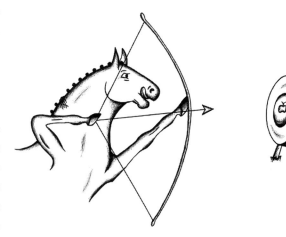

Think BIG. Goals are meant to stretch the imagination, they are meant to go beyond what is reasonable and into what is incredible. If you are able to create big goals which you are passionate about; if you focus on these goals each and every day and if you take action that will move you in the direction of these goals, amazing things will start to happen. You will notice the changes. People around you will notice the changes and the results will come.

Goals are meant to go beyond what is reasonable and into what is incredible

Here goes then, first step is to create your 'big picture'. This is the essence of what you want to do with your horse over, say, the next year or two. Identify these sizeable goals that you want (or need) to achieve. Setting 'big picture' goals gives you the sense of direction that shapes all other aspects of your decision making. Start by just making a statement about what you really want to go after, or maybe a statement outlining the problems you are encountering.

What interests you? What fascinates you? You don't have to know all the details; you can think about the actual goal that you need to set later in a positive and smart way. Just write. Let your imagination take you. Keep writing, let the creative juices flow. Write whatever comes to your mind.

Here are some categories you may wish to consider (or you may have other categories of your own that are important to you).

Relationship With Your Horse

How do you wish your relationship to develop with your horse? What is stopping you from enjoying this? How can this be improved?

Something like 'I need to get my horse to trust me more' or 'I want to understand my horse's behaviours'

Training

Is there any knowledge in particular you want to acquire? What information and skills will you need to have in order to achieve your goals?

Maybe 'learn more about lateral work' or 'I'd like to know more about saddle fitting and it's affect on my horse'

Attitude

Is any part of your mind set holding you back? Is there any part of the way that you behave that upsets you? Are you in the right frame of mind for what you need to do?

Perhaps 'I wish I could develop my ability to focus' or 'I could do with learning to control my emotions'

Physical Capability

Is there anything about your body that is preventing you from moving forward? What level of fitness will you need?

This area is dealt with in great detail later in the book but it could be something like 'I always drop my shoulder on the left' or 'my feet won't stay in the stirrups' or 'I have no stamina'.

Your Horse's Physical Capability

Is your horse physically fit? Are there any issues, dental, muscular, injury? What steps are you going to take to sort this out?

You will already know this and it could be anything from dental checks to lack of flexibility and/or ability to bend.

Riding Level

What level of riding do you wish to attain? Leisure only? Hacking alone or in company? Competition? - What level of competition?

Settle down with some quiet time, a cuppa and a biscuit somewhere you won't be interrupted. You already know on some level what your issues are, you already know what you want but think about each of these categories and begin to write down and build your big picture. Use that time to make some notes; select one or more statements from each category that best reflect what you want to do. As you do this, your first consideration should be for you to make sure that the goals you set are ones you genuinely want to achieve, not ones your parents, family, or anyone else for that matter, might want.

Consider what might be required and when it might be required, in order for you to get where you want to be. Begin to build a picture of how your goal(s) will look.

STEP 2: TRIMMING DOWN, SETTING SMALLER GOALS

Once you have the 'big' picture statements e.g. compete at national level; complete a novice test at home or enter an on-line dressage competition; get my horse safe on hacks. Whatever it might be, you will then begin to set your goals on a number of levels, breaking down each of them into smaller and smaller targets that you must hit in order to reach your ultimate goal.

Look at creating a twelve-month plan of smaller goals that you need to complete if you are to reach your ultimate plan. From there create a nine-month, a six-month, three-month and a one-month plan of progressively smaller goals that will contribute towards the achievement of your ultimate goal. At this stage purely write down what you want to do. Don't even consider how it might be achieved. Break them down so that you have a smaller number of significant goals, then, trim further so that you have a number of really significant goals that you can focus on. Each of these should be based on the previous plan.

Example:	
The Big Picture	Ride a Novice Test
12 Month Plan	Enter the Novice Test

When you get to timescales that are nearer to you, you can get more specific.

9 Month Plan	Consolidate novice work, continue training at Elementary level
6 Month Plans	Develop lateral work and introduce Elementary movements
3 Month Plan	Enter a preliminary test and work on feedback from judge
1 month Plan	Maintain rhythm, straightness, tempo in working paces *
Next Week Plan	Work on trot to canter transitions *
This Week Plan	Run through a Novice test to assess what needs work

*Assumes you have identified these as areas that need working on

In this scenario, the 'this week plan' is the starting point when run through a Novice test to assess where I am in my training then I schedule some time to work on some of the transitions needed for a preliminary test, and so on.

MILESTONES

Once you have a one-month target you could set this as your first milestone. What is the next milestone on the way to your goals? Well, let's say you have a goal to do a preliminary test by month three and to get there you need to achieve a balanced canter by month one. Your month one target is a very valid milestone to achieving your ultimate goal; something that is critical to your success and will really deserve celebrating. You can map out several milestones until you reach your goal. Anything goes, once again what matters is that you write it down and explore. Is there a mini-target you could achieve in one week? What is firing you up? What is giving you a tingling sensation? What is creating a sparkle within you?

The final step in your goal setting activities is your 'to-do-list' of things that you could do today which will begin the work towards your 'big picture' goals. I call this the 'rider focus plan' and it is explained in more depth in Chapter 12 – Do – Rider Focus Plan. At an early stage, your smaller targets might be to read books and gather information, talk to friends about sharing your experiences, information gathering on how you will set about achieving your higher level goals, researching training availability, checking out venues etc. You may even have already found what you are looking for in this book. Once you have your plan, you can start working on it in earnest. Review your plans regularly and make sure that they fit the way in which you want to be with your horse.

SMART GOALS

A useful and long established way of making goals more powerful is to use the S.M.A.R.T. mnemonic. While there are plenty of variants, SMART usually stands for:

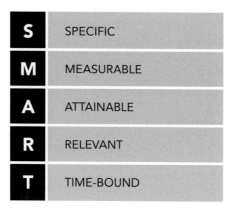

S	SPECIFIC
M	MEASURABLE
A	ATTAINABLE
R	RELEVANT
T	TIME-BOUND

For example, "To compete at the National Championships" is not smart. As a goal, it's more powerful to say …"To compete in the Medium Open Section at the September 20XX National Championships"

Specific	Medium Open Section
Measurable	Class will happen with or without you
Attainable	National Championships (you decide the level that is attainable)
Relevant	This is what you are working towards in your training
Time-bound	September 20XX

Crystal's Goal Setting Tips

1. They have to be yours

Don't just throw something out there because your friend did it once and it sounded good. Consider the most important things you want to get done and then write them down, get excited about them and go into action; if you only have one goal that's great.

2. State them positively

Express each goal as a positive statement. 'Execute trot to halt transitions well' is a much better goal than 'Don't fall into halt from trot.'

3. Be clear-cut

Put in dates, times and amounts so that you can measure achievement. If you do this, you'll know exactly when you have achieved the goal, and can take complete satisfaction from having achieved it. 'Execute a flowing shoulder-in by end of the month' gives you an exercise to work on and a timescale to work towards achieving. You might start by doing a shoulder-in and assessing what problems you are having. Then you might need to ensure that you are asking correctly, by researching on-line (check out The Crystal System Blog at www.likecrystal.com) or asking friends. Your horse may need to build up exercises like shoulder-fore before he is strong enough to do it. You need to get down to the 'nitty gritty' and break down the goal into those baby steps I talked about.

4. Decide priorities

When you have several goals, give each a priority. This helps you to avoid feeling overwhelmed by having too many goals and helps to direct your attention to the most important ones. So 'help my horse to travel better' would be more of a priority than 'attain a certain percentage at a dressage venue'. The travelling issue may be impacting the percentage, so prioritise which should come first.

Crystal's Goal Setting Tips

5. Write them down

This crystallises your goals and gives them more force. It also gives you a point of reference to work with.

6. Keep working goals small

Keep the low-level goals you're working on small and achievable. If the 'this week' or 'this month' goal is too large, then it can seem that you are not making progress towards the 'big picture'. Keeping your daily working goals small and incremental gives more opportunities for reward.

7. Be a realist

It's important to set goals that you can achieve. You may ponder goals that are too difficult because you have not appreciated either the obstacles in the way, or understood quite how much skill you need to develop to achieve a particular level of performance. Be realistic so that you don't disappoint yourself, there is no point in setting 'Ride a Grand Prix' when you have a just backed 4 year old horse.

8. Make adjustments

Re-evaluate your goals, let them go if they no longer hold any attraction

You can and should adjust your goals as they become clearer and you reflect the growth in your knowledge and experiences. Let them go if they no longer hold any attraction. If, for instance your horse gets injured, your goals immediately change to getting him well again. Your focus may change in terms of perhaps increasing your knowledge by reading, attending seminars or clinics, doing some fitness work for yourself etc., instead of actually riding. Don't lose sight of the goal, just find another way to get there and adjust the timescales accordingly. It's just another curve ball and you will get them all the time. A word of warning, if you are not flexible with your goals they can cloud your judgement. Try not to be blinkered. If your horse is telling you that something you are working on is not right, change it.

STAYING ON COURSE

Goals are a funny thing. Not funny hilarious, funny curious. You set them, you write them down, you make picture boards, charts and graphs and tell everyone about them, but the bottom line is that you have to believe in them, you have to want them and they have to be reasonable (and challenging) for you to accomplish. If all of those things are present in your goal setting, you can accomplish anything.

Once you've decided on your goals, keep the process going by reviewing and updating your 'to-do list' on a daily or weekly basis. On a monthly basis, review the longer term plans, and modify them to reflect your changing priorities and experiences. Keep track of your goals through a simple tracking system. This can be as basic as a list or spreadsheet but whatever you decide to use, it should be made use of regularly so you can see where you are in realising your goal and if there are any adjustments to be made. Remember, your tracking system should be a tool to help you follow your progress not an obstacle or an 'Albatross round your neck' which you come to resent. Problem is, without some systematised method of daily accountability, the natural result will be for you to stray off course. Then at the end of the year, you look back and say, "If only…"

Your best of intentions will be dominated by whatever system you have in place. If you have no system, then either old habits or just plain chaos will dominate in the long run, regardless of your intentions and motivation.

It can work really well to think of your goal setting as entering your destination into your own internal G.P.S. (Global Positioning System – like in your satellite navigation system). The destination will remain the same throughout your journey but you may have to change course, take a different path, 'recalculate' your position but you are headed to one final destination, doesn't matter how you get there, just do what works for you.

Crystal's Tip

Share your goals – have an accountability partner

- Sharing your goals with someone is a great idea. It enables you to have an objective person to help you stay on track and increase your motivation to accomplish your goals. Even better, if that someone is slightly more knowledgeable than you and can act as your mentor.

I have already stated 'if you focus on these goals each and every day and if you take action that will move you in the direction of these goals, amazing things will start to happen'. I just wanted to re-iterate the 'take action' bit. Nothing matters until you take action. You simply need to set the target and start moving towards it, in at least some small way, each and every day.

GOAL SETTING EXAMPLES

	GOAL 1 – COMPETITION	
Goal	**Target Date**	**GOAL**
The Big Picture		**Gain Qualification for The 20XX National Dressage Championships at Novice Level**
12 Month Plan	SEPT	National Championships
9 Month Plan	JUN	Regional Championships
6 Month Plan	APR	Qualify for Regional Championships
3 Month Plan	JAN	Be ready for Novice Open Tests
1 Month Plan	SEP	Address any issues with rider focus plan
Next Week	Early AUG	Begin work on rider focus plan
This Week	Early AUG	Complete Rider Focus Plan

GOAL 2– RELATIONSHIP WITH HORSE		
Goal	Target Date	GOAL
The Big Picture		**Have a more relaxed and willing horse within 3 months (identify the issues and list them)**
12 Month Plan	SEPT	Review Progress
9 Month Plan	JUN	Review Progress
6 Month Plan	APR	Continue work and re-evaluate goal
3 Month Plan	JAN	• Desensitising work in the manege • Keep check of handling consistency • Walk in woods • Use massage techniques weekly
1 Month Plan	SEP	• Check consistency in handling – Add to rider focus plan • Walk in woods weekly • Use massage techniques weekly
Next Week	Early AUG	• Schedule walk in woods weekly • Schedule a full body massage weekly
This Week	Early AUG	• Take a walk in woods • Incorporate massage techniques into grooming routine

MY PERSONAL GOALS

NAME:

GOAL 1:

Goal	Target Date	GOAL
The Big Picture		
12 Month Plan		
9 Month Plan		
6 Month Plan		
3 Month Plan		
1 Month Plan		
Next Week		
This Week		

GOAL 2:

Goal	Target Date	GOAL
The Big Picture		
12 Month Plan		
9 Month Plan		
6 Month Plan		
3 Month Plan		
1 Month Plan		
Next Week		
This Week		

GOAL 3:

Goal	Target Date	GOAL
The Big Picture		
12 Month Plan		
9 Month Plan		
6 Month Plan		
3 Month Plan		
1 Month Plan		
Next Week		
This Week		

GOAL 4:

Goal	Target Date	GOAL
The Big Picture		
12 Month Plan		
9 Month Plan		
6 Month Plan		
3 Month Plan		
1 Month Plan		
Next Week		
This Week		

GOAL 5:

Goal	Target Date	GOAL
The Big Picture		
12 Month Plan		
9 Month Plan		
6 Month Plan		
3 Month Plan		
1 Month Plan		
Next Week		
This Week		

You should, by now, know why you are doing this. You know what it is you want to do. You have some tools to keep you on track, now it's time to examine what is needed and that means taking a long hard look at yourself as an athlete. To be 'as one' with your horse you need to match his fitness and athletisism. This question can be broken down into two distinctly different parts. Firstly, are you fit?

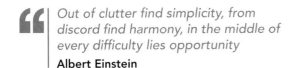

Out of clutter find simplicity, from discord find harmony, in the middle of every difficulty lies opportunity
Albert Einstein

DEFINE – Are you FIT?

Are you fit? If the answer is yes, that's a really good start. But we need to delve deeper, examine the standards by which you are making this judgement?

Establish how you have defined your fitness, because there are many aspects to being fit for horse riding; stamina, strength, agility, flexibility, balance, co-ordination, reaction time and of course your general health.

If the answer is no, then that's also a good start. We all have to start somewhere, right? Might as well be at the bottom. Let's take a look at all the elements combined that will define you as an equestrian athlete, fully able to cope with the rigours of dressage riding and your effectiveness in the saddle.

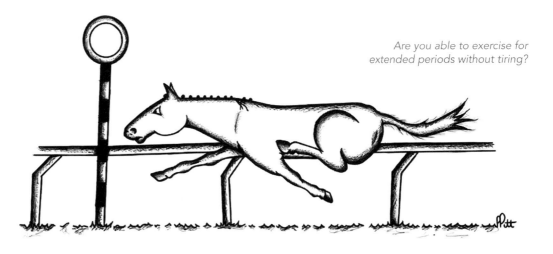

Are you able to exercise for extended periods without tiring?

STAMINA

Are you able to exercise for extended periods without tiring? Stamina relates to your staying power; your aerobic fitness. How efficient is your body at carrying oxygen to your muscles and are your muscles using that oxygen in order for them to continue working efficiently?

Your aerobic capacity can be improved with an awareness of your breathing and how it affects your riding. If, like I was you are 'purple' after a schooling session with a trainer, in need of oxygen and utterly exhausted then you have a way to go. I say after a schooling session with a trainer because rarely do riders put in as much physical effort when they are schooling alone. It is the encouragement by the trainer that tends to galvanise your resilience and fortitude.

Exercise as simple as bouts of brisk walking will help you to improve. I don't know about you but I must walk 10 miles around the yard in any given day (may have exaggerated slightly for effect). My point is this; if I walked to the field to collect my horse more briskly, this simple act will improve my aerobic capacity. If I walk to the hay barn to collect the hay more briskly, this will improve my aerobic capacity. There are a million small, baby steps you can take to improve your aerobic capacity.

Because I was so unfit, aerobically, I undertook a program of walking, jogging and eventually sprinting around the manege for no more than 5 to 10 minutes per day. Absolutely hated it. That is until it started to become easier and I began to feel the benefits. Now I love it. I feel like Rocky Balboa on the days when I find it easy to run around that arena, I really do. It became easier when I started to get control of my breathing. Breathing awareness is a very, very simple and highly effective method of overcoming all sorts of difficulties and the key to improving any stamina issues. I go into this more in Chapter 7 – DISCOVER – The Beauty In Your Body. Just be aware for now that breathing 'properly' is effortless.

STRENGTH

How quickly do your muscles get fatigued? Muscular strength endurance is the ability to carry out work under resistance without tiring. It may require some specialist input, but resistance training will strengthen any weak muscles you may have. Of course, if you have an injury or have just recovered from injury you should seek medical advice. If you feel you have a weakness, get in touch with a specialist sports coach and/or physiotherapist to help you build strength. Let's be candid here, we really don't want to have bodies like Adonis, but we do need strength. So, assuming you are good to go, the area in which most strength is needed when you ride is in the centre of the body.

Core stability relates to the part of the body surrounded by the abdominal wall, the pelvis, lower back and diaphragm and its ability to stabilise the body during movement. And guess what? The diaphragm is the main muscle used for breathing and so breathing is important in providing the necessary core stability for moving and we can all breathe, that's easy peasy.

The core is associated with the abdominal muscle groups and stability is associated with strength. However, the core actually consists of the abdominal muscle groups, together with the hip abductors/adductors, hip flexors, and lumbar spine. It is commonly believed that core stability is essential for the maintenance of an upright posture and especially for movements that require extra effort such as riding. Given that it is the lumbar spine that is primarily responsible for posture and stability and for providing the strength needed for stability, especially when utilised in dynamic sports like riding, it is vital that when you consider the 'core' you consider the whole central region of the body.

Without core stability the lower back is not supported from inside and can be injured by strain caused by exercise. It is also believed that insufficient core stability can result in lower back pain, poor posture and lethargy. However and here's the bombshell, there is little support in research for many of the benefits attributed to specific core muscle exercises. Trunk or core specific exercising has failed to demonstrate preventative benefits against injuries in sports or indeed to improve sports performance. What has been proven is that at best core stability training has the same benefits as general, non-specific exercise like, would you believe, walking? There it is, to improve your core strength, get walking (briskly) and whilst you are walking, breathe. Yes, simplicity IS the key to brilliance. Clear?

AGILITY

Described as the ability to change the position or direction of the body rapidly, agility is also influenced by balance, co-ordination, position of centre of gravity, speed and skill. Your agility for riding can only really be improved by practicing specifically for dressage. You can weave in and out of cones and zip around an agility course as much as you like, but it is the ability of your upper and lower body to move independently of each other that is fundamental to your riding. Nothing you do on the ground will improve the ability of each independent part of your body to act alone in the dynamic situation of absorbing the movement of a horse. Saddle time is the only answer if you have agility issues.

Bottom line is that using the legs should not have any effect whatsoever on the upper body … so, just how agile are you?

FLEXIBILITY

Do all your joints have the capacity to move through their full range of motion? Joint stiffness is usually associated with injury (or age!). For example, if you sit all day in your work, the flexibility of your hip joints may not be sufficient to enable you to be effective in the saddle. So, consider just how flexible are you?

Put aside your riding aspirations, your quality of life will be much enhanced by improving and maintaining a good range of motion in your joints. Gender, age, and genetics are important considerations for the range of motion you can achieve. However regular stretching exercises can and will improve flexibility, whenever it is started. When you move onto the section of the book called 'The Beauty In Your Body', your weaknesses in terms of flexibility will begin to come to the forefront. If you are flexibly fit, this whole process is going to be so much easier for you, if not, take steps to identify the issues and get there soonest.

BALANCE

Is there room for improvement in your balance? Your ability to stay upright or stay in control of your body movements, balance is a very important component of dressage. But balance isn't just using 'body sense' to stay upright or absorb movements, we use our eyes, ears, touch, in fact all of the senses to help retain our balance.

There are two types of balance: static and dynamic. Static balance is maintaining stability when stationary, while dynamic balance is maintaining stability and symmetry when moving. Dynamic balance is an important component of agility. Clearly it is the mastery of dynamic balance that is all important in your riding. For those of you truly dedicated to the sport or for that matter mental and physical fitness, the martial art of Tai Chi is the way forward to improve your balance.

CO-ORDINATION

We all know the 'pat your head and rub your tummy' co-ordination test, but can you do it? The ability to move two or more body parts under control, smoothly and efficiently is all about your ability to co-ordinate the said parts. Co-ordination is a complex skill that requires good levels of other fitness components such as balance, strength and agility.

Motor co-ordination is achieved when the movements of several body parts are combined in a manner that is well timed, smooth, and efficient. You will already have heard about giving co-ordinated aids, so you will know the importance of co-ordination in your riding. It is difficult skill to teach and only comes with saddle time and practise, having said that, learning to co-ordinate is all about having the right techniques. Even the 'pat your head and rub your tummy' test has a proven technique that works.

Start off patting your head. Get to the rhythm and the beat of the 'Thump, Thump, Thump'. Focus just on that.

Stop patting your head and start rubbing your tummy in circle motions. Focus just on rubbing your tummy. 'Swish, Swash, Swish, Swash'.

Now depending on you, (you'll find out sooner or later) see which (rubbing your tummy or patting your head) feels more dominant.

Now on the less dominant one, focus your mind there.

Slowly start the other one, still keeping most of your mind power on the less dominant one. You may fail at first but don't give up. Keep on practising.

Here's another quick fun thing to prove that co-ordination can be overridden by your brains pre-programmed operating system. This will confuse your mind and you will keep trying over and over again to see if you can outsmart your foot, but, you cannot.

Crystal Says

Hehehe, it did, didn't it?

While sitting at your desk in front of your computer, lift your right foot off the floor and make clockwise circles.

Now, while doing this, draw the number '6' in the air with your right hand. Your foot will change direction.

Co-ordination is also about your ability to time your aids. I often tell a tale about my 'eureka moment' when learning shoulder fore off the bend. The milliseconds it was taking me to do the aids one at a time in sequence did not have the desired effect. Coordinating them so that I executed the aids all together, in the same moment, at the same time, all at once meant I achieved a flowing shoulder fore.

How well can you co-ordinate your body parts to give your horse fair and effective aids?

REACTION TIME

How quick do you react to a stimulus? When you begin training for dressage your horse's reactions will be much quicker than yours. As you progress you will catch up, then your horse will go in front of you and you will catch up again. The cycle continues until you train your reaction time to be 'one step ahead' of your horse and you are able to react instantly and instinctively. Another skill that comes with practice, but you can improve your reaction times by working through what you need to do on the ground, until it becomes automatic when you are in the saddle.

Is your brain fit for this? Well, don't worry if not the next chapter will help.

GENERAL HEALTH

Who would have thought that Dressage required so much stamina and fitness? Let us not forget your general health. Do you have any issues that are holding you back from achieving your desired goals in dressage? See your Doctor before embarking on any fitness regime if you have a history of illness that may affect your ability to undertake the work involved, safely.

Answering the above questions truthfully and identifying where you may need to concentrate your work efforts can help you to set a few goals, both short and long term.

Do you have any health issues that are hindering your progress?

Crystal's Tip

- You may have plenty of stamina but your coordination might require some work. By targetting short term work on your balance you can set a longer term goal of improving your coordination. So the short term goal would be 'do some walking to improve core strength' or 'buy a balance ball and sit on it one hour a week watching TV'. Think outside of the box and get creative about how you can overcome your fitness issues.

THE CRYSTAL SYSTEM

DEFINE YOUR FITNESS LEVELS & IDENTIFY IMPROVEMENT OPPORTUNITIES

STAMINA	
STRENGTH	
AGILITY	
FLEXIBILITY	
BALANCE	
CO-ORDINATION	
REACTION TIME	
GENERAL HEALTH	

Now you know how fit, or otherwise you might be, before you go setting yourself goals to be a superfit, gymnastic, speed demon of an athlete with a rippling six-pack consider the purpose of your fitness. The next chapter brings it all into perspective, by helping you to identify just what is the purpose and how far you need to go.

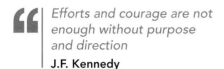

*Efforts and courage are not
enough without purpose
and direction*
J.F. Kennedy

DEFINE – Are you FIT FOR PURPOSE?

Are you fit for purpose? Perhaps you're not sure about this, but knowing the purpose of what you are striving towards will surely help.

There is no need to be able to run a marathon to be able to ride well, on the other hand you do need to be able to trot or canter a horse for half an hour without needing oxygen or turning scarlet in the face. For me the purpose of my training is to be 'as one' with my horse. To get and keep that elusive sense of harmony. Breaking it down further, the purpose is to get that feeling to stay with me, at all times whilst riding. This is the reason why I train. Define your purpose and then consider whether you have the physical attributes necessary to realise that purpose. Being 'as one' means no resistance between horse and rider, for me this meant I had to really take a good look at my body's ability to flex and stretch and balance and co-ordinate. It fell well short, so I embarked on a series of exercises to help hone my body (and in particular my pelvis and hips) so that they were fit for purpose. This is a work in progress, but improvement is the goal and improvement is what I am getting.

There can be few people who do not know the benefits of stretching before exercise

There can be few people who do not know about and understand the benefits of stretching before exercise. There will be few people who do not stretch their horse and allow a warm up for the horse before a training session. Why then are we not prepared to put a little effort into our own bodies? I knew and understood the logic and yet I did not stretch my own muscles before riding for many years. Why, is this? I have concluded that I am lazy! I had to lie on the floor, or have an exercise ball or do it at some other time than that allocated for my horses (i.e. when I was at the stables) it just did not happen. Not until I embarked on this journey did I fully understand the significance of flexibility and muscle strength and fitness to my riding. I did not appreciate how disadvantaged I was with the negative muscle memory from years sitting at a desk, or the way my shoulder hindered me because of the riding injury I had sustained 17 years earlier.

So in years gone by when I was told 'get your heels down' I would push down with my calf, sending tension up through my thigh, pinching with my knees, raising my seatbones out of the saddle, tilting me forward and unbalancing my position and of course getting in the way of progress. However, since recognising that the tightness in my Psoas muscles was never going to allow me to 'push down into my heels' without the catalogue of issues described above, what I actually needed was a few simple and easy to do exercises that I could spend 10 mins doing which released my Psoas muscles. Then, when my mentor wanted a more level heel from me he would simply say 'heels' which is the cue to me to relax my lower back, open my hip angle and lift my toes, giving the desired result of level heels, job done.

You may not have the body issues I had: you may have stamina issues, which means that you might have to look at the way in which you breathe to make it easier for yourself. Or maybe it's your mental health that is letting you down and you need to sharpen up your thinking. In any event, consider what it is you want, what level you want to achieve, how often you will ride, what levels of fitness are needed to get you to a novice level and beyond. Understand the purpose of what you are doing and take the necessary action to achieve it.

THE CRYSTAL SYSTEM

What is your Purpose?

Does Your Fitness match?

Let's have a quick recap and summarise what hopefully, you will have learnt so far.

You have established what is motivating you or rather, why you want this.

You understand that being clear about what you want is important.

You will be considering your big picture and working to pull together some goals.

You have taken some time to assess your physical ability in terms of fitness and know how far you need to go with fitness for the purpose of your riding.

What you have not done yet is learnt anything about how to ride. This is a very pertinent point and I bring this up now because what I discovered in my quest to become a skillfull rider is that a very large proportion of what the top riders do is work related to getting their mind and body fit for purpose. All this assessment, planning, re-assessment and pondering will culminate into a full understanding of how your body is, or is not working when you elegantly mount your steed. This is sadly lacking in the mind-set of the grassroots rider and accounts for 90% of failures. For those of you that want to rush off and ride, do so. Go and have a go, just please ensure that you follow the rest of the program and keep in your mind that patience is a virtue that you must have to succeed in dressage.

The Discovery phase of the programme is next. It too is in two parts and takes a more in depth look at your mind and body and it's suitability for riding dressage.

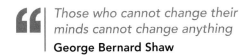

Those who cannot change their minds cannot change anything
George Bernard Shaw

DISCOVER – Clarity in your Thinking

The way you approach your riding is fundamental to the realisation of your dream. Not only it's realisation but also whether or not you enjoy the process.

Dressage is a thinking sport, riding is about strategy. Ask yourself what is the most valuable aid when riding? The answer is not your legs, or your contact, or your seat, it is your brain and how quickly you are able to process the huge amount of information you need to ride and perform dressage and indeed work your body at the same time. You have to be quick and sharp. In a dressage test there are a succession of movements, one after the other, all requiring different thought processes, aids, body movements in which the aim is to seem to do as little as possible.

We have already talked about goal setting and its potential benefits in allowing you to follow the process of building a road-map to your ultimate goal and how this is possibly the most influential tool you have for helping you choose where you want to be, getting focus and crystallising your thinking. By knowing precisely what you want to achieve, you know where you have to concentrate all those considerable efforts you are putting in and quickly spot any distractions that can, and so easily do, lead you astray. However, you may still feel uncertain and lacking sufficient clarity in your thoughts about your future direction. What if you can't decide what you need to do next? What if you can't formulate an achievable goal? What if I set myself off on the wrong track? Fortunately for you there are a number of actions you can take and mental adjustments you can make that will help you shift from uncertainty to certainty.

First of all, do not assume that clarity is something that will arrive in good time if you wait long enough. Unfortunately it is not something bestowed from above. As with everything worth having it takes a little work. Clarity is a decision. Whilst I am an advocate of finding your own way and taking many influences in your dressage journey, at some point you will need to decide your direction and dedicate yourself to that way of working. In my experience, when you begin your journey, if you remain open to lots of different training methods at the same time, you get confusion and fuzziness, but when you commit yourself to one specific direction, clarity is the natural result.

If you are anything like I was, it is entirely possible that you may not be very good at creating clarity for yourself at this stage. Indeed, you may be very good at creating confusion and uncertainty for yourself. Do not despair, for now all you need to do is simply acknowledge and take ownership of the fact that it is definitely you who is creating your current level of clarity (or not). Furthermore, realize and accept that if you are going to move forward in your riding then you must actively make some changes.

You need to stop creating the opposite of clarity for yourself. For example if you consume too much mind-numbing junk food and alcohol; if you over stimulate yourself with caffeine (which leads to racing thoughts); if you get easily distracted with excessive TV or waste your time complaining that you don't know what to do – just stop it. Make the decision to stop spinning in unproductive circles and give yourself some space to create and enjoy clarity. The bottom line is this, either you feel clear and focused right now, or you don't. Clarity is more than just a feeling, it's an emotion, a vibe, and it is a powerful state of being to experience and is therefore, worth having a go at.

Have a go at a visualisation method. Sit quietly for a few moments and imagine what it's like to be a skilled rider. Imagine what your surroundings would be like if you were an assured rider with skills that others admire. Imagine those people and how you would interact with them. Imagine which breeches you would wear, how you'd move, and how you'd communicate. Paint yourself a vivid picture of this reality in which you feel crystal clear about the direction that your riding is taking. What matters are not the specifics of the visualisation that you create but soaking up the feeling it is giving you. Hold it close for future reference. Bear in mind that it is you that is 100% responsible for your level of clarity, you can use trainers and advice givers like myself as a resource to help you see the big picture, but don't give your power away. If you try to give your power away to such people, hoping they'll tell you what to do, it will backfire. You will become frustrated. Just as I did.

THE CRYSTAL SYSTEM: VISUALISATION

Where are you?	
What are you wearing?	
What is your manner like?	
Who is with you?	
What are you saying?	
What are you doing?	
What is happening around you?	

HOW DO YOU FEEL?

I understand you may need help, because sometimes it's tough to set a clear goal because you don't know what you're getting into. If this is the case you can experiment in order to gain clarity about the goal you're exploring. Doing what you're already doing certainly won't give you more clarity but thinking about what to do next and writing down some goals can certainly help, but that isn't always enough. Sometimes you have to get moving before clarity can be achieved. Remember the baby steps I talked about? You may enjoy more clarity about where you are going, once you are underway. So take a tip or two of mine into the arena, have a go, see where it takes you and then begin thinking about the bigger picture.

Don't wait for clarity to come to you. You're responsible for creating your own clarity from within. To be a 'mindful rider' you need to be alert and focused, constantly evaluate and re-evaluate the merits of what you do. A non-thinking rider is mindless, mechanical, senseless; (as I was!) proof can be found in the rider that stubbornly sticks to one solution, even if it does not appear to be working (as I did!). You need to take steps to increase your awareness; think about why the exercises and skills you need are important; learn why you need to do what it is you intend to do; take responsibility for yourself; keep track of your goals; try to be open to different and creative problem solving; be in charge of your own riding destiny.

Don't wait for clarity to come to you

It takes time to develop confidence in your own decision making and problem solving ability. Just as it takes time to exercise the muscles of the body so it takes time to exercise the brain. Don't be too harsh on yourself if you don't think you have developed these skills yet, it will come. You will get quicker. The catch 22 comes when you begin to develop your ability to think quicker, only to find that your horse is still one step ahead. That happens as your training progresses they will always keep pushing your boundaries, enjoy the ride, it's very rewarding.

Simply put, in the arena you should be the only part of the team that knows what is happening or where you are going. Nothing breaks the confidence or concentration of a horse more effectively than not bothering to prepare him for a movement. Your horse is taken by surprise and goes into self-preservation mode when he sees the wall looming up in front of him. We use the half-halt to bring our horse to attention; to prepare him for things to come; to make him aware that something is about to happen. It is absolutely vital that you prepare your horse in sufficient time to be able to allow him to carry out the movement and whilst you are still in that movement, prepare for the next. Not easy, but for me the revelation came when calling a test for a friend. If you were calling a test for a friend and on the point at which they reached the 'A' marker you shouted out "A Enter at Working Trot", they would not be able to turn into the arena on time and they probably wouldn't be your friend for long either. Take a moment to equate in your mind the way you would call a test to the time you and your horse need to prepare for each movement, grab a beverage of your choice and think about this for a while, maybe run through a test. Really give some consideration to how much time you need to prepare each movement and take that into the arena with you next time you ride. Help your horse by giving him the time he needs to prepare. You are a team, he needs your help.

Crystal's Tip

- Your horse will work for maybe an hour a day, is it really too much to expect him to be attentive to you and work to some degree for the whole hour? One of the things that helped me most in developing the correct mind-set for my training sessions is to think 'Clock on – Clock off'. As I enter the arena, we are training and we clock on. As I exit the arena, we are done so we can clock off.

Horses have been part of human's history for centuries. A system of training was first documented by the Greek Cavalry Officer Xenophon, as horses had to be obedient and manoeuvrable for battle. So in time horsemanship became an art and the first riding school was set up in Naples in 1532 by Federica Grisone. Dressage in its original form was developed as a test of the horse's obedience. Your training should demonstrate that your horse is obedient to your aids. But in order for you to expect your horse to be obedient and responsive you will need to understand how he can most comfortably carry you. A horse which is not able to carry the rider properly will become tense and uncomfortable and likely to be evasive and disobedient. To assess obedience in your horse you must assess your riding. Be very clear with your aids. Before you ride, revisit in your mind the aids you will apply for each movement and check for yourself once on board that you are actually executing them as intended. Sometimes we do something for so long it becomes ingrained and a little sloppy. A well-worn analogy is your car driving. Is it as accurate as it was the day you took your test? No, of course it isn't. In order to be as accurate as the day you took your test you would have to put some serious thought into what you are doing when you are driving. Fact is that you have reached 'unconscious competence' in your driving ability and now you do the absolute minimum required to keep you safe.

You will, without doubt, be heavily penalised by the judges if do not execute the shapes within your test accurately. Accuracy of the shapes you make in the arena are essential if you are not going to drop marks you could easily hold onto. Accuracy is a basic requirement of dressage and never the fault of your horse. So, how do you get those all important circles, turns, diagonals and loops into your work routine as second nature? A simple yet effective method is to never do any shape in the arena that you would not find in a dressage test. Condition yourself to be true, so for example ride a true circle be that 8m 10m 15m or 20m – (never 9m), even when you are relaxing your horse and taking a break, you should ensure that when you give your horse a loose rein and are meandering around the arena it is in a shape

If you always do what you've always done, you'll always get what you've always got
Henry Ford

that you would see in the dressage test. Change the rein across the diagonal or with a half circle and back to the track, it is all part of the conditioning of you and your horse to the shapes required in a test and teaching your horse to listen and be in-tune with you whatever you are doing, even when you are having a break. If you are walking around the outside track, you are making a square and should use your corners, even though you are not actively in training mode, if you are relaxing you are still training, basically if you are in the arena, you are training.

Have you ever ridden a problem, time and time again and thought 'he always goes off the circle at that point' or 'whenever I ride past that point he loses rhythm' or 'he always drops his shoulder on that corner'. If the answer is yes (and it was for me) then do something about it. I truly hope I am the only one who, despite knowing the Henry Ford quote *"If you always do what you've always done, you'll always get what you've always got"* I would go round focussed on something else (that's my excuse) and wonder why I keep getting the same result, until Mark would say in a fairly exasperated manner, 'Change something. You know that your horse is going to baulk at that corner, so next time round prepare for it, do a little shoulder-fore, more inside leg, half-halt, just do something to, at least try, and solve the problem! OK?' When someone points out something obvious like that it's hard not to feel a little foolish, isn't it? The Henry Ford quote is so very wise and well worth remembering when you have trudged the same path for many years and feel a lack of achievement, it may be that it's time to try a different approach; to experiment and explore.

If clarity is a decision then as indicated earlier at some point you will need to decide your direction; to be clear in your thinking you need to …

Visualise your success
Increase your awareness
Learn to think quicker
Give the time needed to execute each movement
Assess the way you apply the aids
Ensure accuracy at all times in your movements
Do something different with recurring errors
Clock on and clock off each training session

Next question – Is your body beautiful? You don't have to answer that one, of course it is. But is it beautiful on a horse?

Crystal Says

Let's discover the beauty in your body.

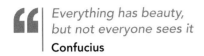

Everything has beauty,
but not everyone sees it
Confucius

DISCOVER - The Beauty in your Body

Of course, being an athlete is not just about fitness, the elegant, calm and quiet position we all aspire to have is beautiful, aesthetically and functionally. For me the very essence of why it is so beautiful is because of effectiveness.

There are riders who look pretty, but do not communicate with their horse; there are riders who believe themselves to be effective but will also admit to 'a few positional faults'. I do not hold with either of these schools of thought. I want to be able to influence my horse with my riding whilst having a correct seat. This for me is where the beauty is.

I remember the day Mark Bentley first chanced upon his trainer Spencer Wilton. We were at the Winter Championships and we were there with a group of my female friends, unsurprisingly he decided to wander off on his own. When he came back he was pretty excited. He had attended the

Discover the beauty in your body

event with the specific purpose of finding a trainer and had seen a rider that he described as 'beautiful on a horse' so he rushed off when the rider came to a halt. Spencer's partner at the time was Carl Hester who was standing on the side-lines; Mark approached 'excuse me, do you mind if I just speak with the rider?' he asked 'Do you train riders?' Spencer shot a puzzled looked at Carl, 'yes' he replied.

'Will you train me?' Mark asked. A short conversation about where he was at with his riding and what his horse was like ensued followed by 'Well, here's my number, give me a call and we'll discuss it' from Spencer.

Mark found us a little further down the working in arena and enthusiastically explained that he had spoken to the rider, who was 'with that guy over there'. We looked over and were incredulous, 'that's Carl Hester and Spencer Wilton' I said. Mark knew of these elite riders, of course, but had not been into dressage long enough to be able to recognise them. We all laughed at his audacity and he promptly went back over to apologise to Carl for not acknowledging him properly. Anyway, the point is, it is the elegant, calm and quietly effective position that Spencer Wilton demonstrates that is the dream. He is an outstanding example of how to sit.

To begin the process of examining your own body and ability to sit correctly, you need to grasp one essential ethos; whether you are training at the very highest level or a beginner in the sport ask yourself 'is it me or is it my horse?' This basic question never goes away, even for the most experienced rider. To answer this ever present question you should automatically run through a check list related to your basic position. The majority of problems rider's face when working their horses (hollowing, rushing, lack of forward urge, no bend, over bent, crookedness etc.) can usually be traced to the rider's incorrect position. So for example, a faulty contact will be the result of a lack of co-ordination and it will be a positional fault that won't allow correct co-ordination.

There can be no rider on the planet that is not aware of the ear, shoulder, hip, and heel alignment requirement (except maybe complete beginners) and in my research I have found that there is no credible system of riding that does not advocate that this is necessary. I am not about to say anything different. It is essential, full stop. My only observation is that whilst every system, method and trainer recognises its importance, very few do what is needed to realistically help a rider achieve this ultimate position or set it as a critical goal in their technique. This is evident from the riding I see at lower level dressage events. They should, it is one of the single decisive elements to becoming a skilful rider and is the first and foremost task you should focus on.

So, how do we do this? The first thing is to discover the restrictions that your body is putting on achieving the ear/shoulder/hip/heel aligned position. Perhaps, like me, your hips are too closed, your Achilles tendon is too tight, you are not sitting on your seat-bones, your back is not able to relax, and your shoulders are rounded (I was in a pretty bad way wasn't I?) and hopefully you will have explored some of these things in the 'Define your Fitness' chapter of the book. If so, you will already be making plans or even working towards relaxing and loosening any issues your body may have.

Looking in more detail at the most effective position that elite riders use, in this chapter I have started at the top and worked down the rider's body, giving you some insights as to what you can look for, some exercises to maybe address what you find and some tips to help you along the way. There is a lot of information here, probably too much to take in, in one go. My best advice is that you read through and identify your main issues, formulate some goals to help you overcome them and use the rest of the section as a reference guide to be revisited periodically.

HEAD AND NECK

Your head is essentially a 10 to 15 pound bowling ball at the top of your neck. Good head alignment means that you use a minimum amount of muscular effort to hold up your head, allowing the skeleton to do most of the work. When your head is well-aligned front to back, you can lengthen through your spine all the way through the top of your head, thereby countering the downward force of gravity.

Align your head and neck, counter the downward force of gravity

Do you have any difficulty looking where you are going when riding?

Does your head tilt or stray from the optimum point that is to be looking over your horse's ears?

Do you find your neck (and shoulders) are tense when you ride, or maybe a little stiff afterward?

Do you have difficulty sitting the trot?

The solution may be all in your head. Far too many riders look down at their horse whilst riding. When riding dressage movements you should ideally look approximately two metres in front of where you are directing your horse to go, through his ears. So, if you are on a circle, look up and in front, not down and certainly not across the circle. Why? Because you will be putting unnecessary pressure on your ability to balance and be in harmony with your horse and if your horse is particularly sensitive you will be giving him signals to slow or stop if you tip the balance of your body forward.

Crystal's Tip

- How to find a good comfortable head position. Lengthen your neck so that your head moves slightly upward. Think of 'pricking your ears' as if you were a horse. Feel the shoulders go back, turn your head slowly, left and right. Is it easy? Do you have any stiffness or restriction in the movement? Do you feel any change in your seat? If you are attentive you may feel your hip angle open as your seat deepens.

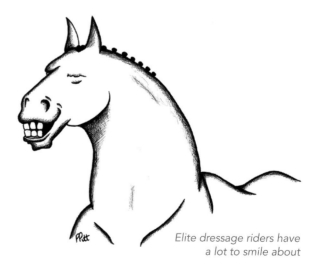

Elite dressage riders have a lot to smile about

- I'd like to bet that the majority of riders enjoy their riding. Yet how often do you see a smile on the face of a rider whilst training? A very simple and hugely beneficial tip is to relax the lower part of your face; smile from the inside, it will help you relax your shoulders and arms. Often we don't even know we are doing it, but when concentrating, the effort involved shows as tension in the jaw muscles. Elite dressage riders have a lot to smile about, but maybe it's actually because they smile a lot. If smiling is too difficult for you (?) simply open or drop the lower jaw slightly (do not allow it to hang open and try not to dribble).

- Whenever you feel 'stuck' simply take a second to 'prick your ears' and free your whole body

- In a test, don't forget that all important smile at the judge.

ARMS AND SHOULDERS

Now I am not a student of the classical masters, but one of the things (and there are many others) that I notice about the classical masters photographs is the way they hold their arms. Or should I say the way their arms look so soft and effortless. You get the sense that all the messages are coming just from the fingers.

The fact is that the arms are only attached to the trunk by the clavicle (collar bone) and of course the muscles, ligaments and tendons of the rotator cuff, which is known as the shoulder girdle. If you have strong core muscles but your shoulder girdle is weak you will struggle to relax the hands due to the lack of control of the upper limb at the scapular (shoulder blade).

Years of bending over a computer has left me with a tendency to round my shoulders. A fractured left clavicle (the horse rider's injury) which did not heal well, means I am unable to keep a correct alignment of my shoulder girdle without me actually thinking about it as, in its 'natural stance' it is crooked and twisted. I was told once that since I had decided to do something about it I was a recovering 'slumper', which appeals to my sense of drama about the whole thing. Commonly riders round their shoulders forward and collapse

Crystal's Tips

- At the walk, shake out each arm to literally shake away the tension, then take a deep breath (which will relax, lift and open your chest) and at the same time roll your shoulders up toward your ears, then push them back and down. Repeat this exercise whenever you feel your shoulder muscles tense as if pulling your shoulders up.

- A very simple 'off the horse' shoulder alignment self-check is to stand in front of a mirror in your most natural and comfortable position. Look at your hands:
  - Can you see one thumb and the index finger?
  - Can you see more?
  - Can you see the thumb, 1st Finger and 2nd Finger?
  - Can you see the back of the hand?
  - Do your arms rest in front of your body?
  - If you can see more than the thumb and first finger or if your arms rest in front of your body, you will have an internal shoulder rotation which is typically described as rounded shoulders and this will, without doubt, be affecting your riding position. An easy fix is to face your palms up (thumbs facing rearward) and move your arms back to behind your seat. Do this all day, no one will notice. It helps with shoulder posture.

their chest thus sending the entire centre of gravity ahead of their horse. Tension wires itself to the arms and forearm muscles visibly tighten. It spreads like a disease through the body, knees clutch, sending heels up and the lower legs back. With hunched body and dropped chin, breathing becomes a chore. I have to confess here that although this scenario sounds far-fetched, it actually happened to me. I found myself 'out of breath' and in a state of anxiety (particularly in the canter) with very shallow breathing, on more than one occasion. The shoulders need to be relaxed back and down, with the chest expanded. The starting point is the 'pricking ears' exercise for the head. This helps the shoulders 'fall' back into position. Try not to open the chest by pulling the shoulder blades tighter together. Firstly keep the shoulder blades as wide as possible then expand your chest. You will feel taller, but still supple through the upper torso and at the same time you will have lifted your diaphragm which will enable you to breathe more deeply and correctly. Rounded shoulders make it impossible to use your upper body effectively on your horse.

HANDS AND WRISTS

As humans we depend greatly on our hands. Our arms and hands are our first line of defence for balancing ourselves in everyday life. Instinct can take over and force you to use your hands for balance. Sometimes it is the overly aggressive use of the reins that is the problem and once a rider understands that they cannot force a horse to do something with excessive rein aids the problem is halfway solved. Hanging onto the reins for balance is not entirely the fault of the hands. The hands only come into play as other balance mechanisms fail. The problem is inevitably elsewhere. You will not be able to develop good hands if you are experiencing balance problems elsewhere because as a human you will use your hands for balance.

If you are having issues with heels coming up and ankles being tense, you will also be having problems with your hands; if your lower back is stiff and unable to flex the movement has to come out somewhere, usually the hands; if your shoulders are rigid, guess what? … problem with the hands.

Stop for a minute and think about what you are doing with your hands. The reins are an extension of your arms, the bit runs through your horse's mouth.

Crystal's Tips

- Look at the overall picture, find the 'root cause' of the problem and address it. As a rider you will never be able to develop good hands if you are unable to support them with a great seat and legs and be in complete harmony with your horse, which in turn leaves the hands completely independent. Practice mostly doing nothing. Make adjustments when you feel the need, then go back to doing nothing.

- In trot, gradually allow your reins to be taken down through your hands until you have a loose rein, continue trotting until you are on the buckle end. If you begin to feel unbalanced, you have some work to do.

- Why not test yourself on the lunge with a friend and just see whether you have a reliance on the reins, many of you, even established competition riders will be surprised at how your balance is affected without reins. This will tell you how much work you have to do.

- Think about having a workspace for your hands that is no bigger than 12 cubic inches in front of you. Your hands should never come out of this workspace.

- Good riding gloves allow for a subtler, finer grip on the reins.

From the moment you pick up the reins you become responsible for being kind and consistent with your hands. Be aware of the power that your hands have over your horse's mouth, and be conscious to avoid being overly harsh. Imagine that you could reach down and hold on to the bit rings. Would you see-saw and pull? Would you be inconsistent in the way you hold the bit rings, constantly jabbing the sides of the mouth? No, of course you wouldn't, so you must ensure your hands are closed in a soft but firm fist to avoid unnecessary communications.

The goal is to maintain a smooth, elastic and quiet communication regardless of what your horse is doing. Often using your arms and hands to fix a problem or to accomplish your goal is so instinctive that you don't even realise that this is the very thing that is the cause of the problem. Instinct is very powerful, as is habit; the combination of instinct and habit will result in the over-use of the hands. You need to make the habit a good one. When it comes to hands and wrists you should throw away the rulebook. It has a conflicting effect to 'good hands' to put too much effort into having your hands and forearms exactly as per the rulebook.

This puts unnecessary pressure on you to be correct, stifling your ability to feel. Instead concentrate on ensuring that your shoulders and upper arms are relaxed and your hands will follow.

Consider whether your hands are 'tuned-in' to the rest of your body. You are asking to extend, collect, turn – are your hands working in conjunction with the rest of your body and offering your horse a truly connected question and response? Thumbs should have a slight bend in them to defer a 'dead' feeling through the rein to your horse. Straight wrists means hands that are angled towards each other and give the appearance of being somewhat rounded, because the back of the hand is on the same straight line as the arm. The reins should be held in the first third of the fingers, where the fingers join the hand, with closed fingers, keeping them soft, so not clamped closed. The feeling should be easy and effortless.

If you find that you are prone to letting your reins slip longer then you are probably either riding with the reins on the fingertips or your hand is too loose and the thumb is not sat on top of the rein. Another of my 'eureka moments' came when I began to hold the reins correctly! Instinctively, I could hold the reins without them slipping through my fingers, I could keep a consistent contact, and my horse was much steadier in her way of going as a result. I had to remember to push the reins up into that final third of my fingers but it really was a revelation.

Good hands are the result of a good frame of mind. This being the case, your mind has to know when to resist and when to give. This is at the very moment your horse gives. Use your hands intermittently. Be still as soon as your horse answers and only use them again if something changes and you need a correction. Ask. If your horse does not react, stop and immediately start again. If he gives, you give and then immediately cease all action, thereby keeping the stability required to allow your horse forward. Try not to be frustrated if your hands seem to have a mind of their own, quite often you may not even realise that you have set your hands and arms. Simply making a conscious effort to soften the arms and keep the joints supple and flexible can correct this.

ELBOWS

Communicating effectively with your horse is not just about the hands, it is the action of the arms that allow the hands to be 'good.' The irony is that if you have to think too much about what to do with your arms and hands they can be reactive and behind the motion. Combine tight shoulders, looking down, a collapsed tummy and tight hips with the aforementioned and you will realise why you are having problems schooling your horse.

Nonsensically, developing non-thinking communication that instinctively does what is needed will take a lot of thought. Almost everyone, at some time, will have difficulty with how to use their hands. Learning to give in a way that is valuable to your riding is a real skill. Done correctly an onlooker would never be able to see you give, however, they would clearly see your horse's reaction to the give as he becomes rounder and softer and strides out. All too often riders think that a 'give' is a 'throw away' of the rein contact. It is not. It is a softening of the hand. Known as the 'descente de main' in classical riding, the give is essentially to stop actively using the hand.

Crystal's Tips

- As indicated earlier, from the shoulder the upper arm should hang straight down by your side, to a well bent elbow. Try and release all of the tension from the base of the neck, across the back of the shoulders, down the upper arm and out of the elbow. With the central part of the upper body as tall as possible this should all hang gently down. (Most riders say that they are riding with a really soft contact because they feel their hands are still and fingers are mobile, but if, from the neck down to the elbow is tight, as with most riders, then your horse will quickly learn to lean or pull against the rider).

- When we say 'give' we mean relax only, we do not mean throw the reins forward and 'give' them, the give is from the elbow, no more than an inch.

BREATHING

Without question the most underestimated, undervalued, unappreciated, under-rated tool in a rider's toolbox is breathing. I should know I am guilty of not tapping into the power that correct breathing gives you. I have been told to learn to breathe properly and virtually ignored the advice. I can't tell you why, it seems that I know best and I consider being advised to breathe as no advice at all.

How many of you are now thinking "Wow, that's a real corker, I'll give that a go"? I'll wager not many of you. However, now that I understand clearly the benefits of 'good' breathing I have to say that I am more than a little miffed with myself that I didn't take it more seriously much earlier in my training and have been looking around for someone to blame for not instilling in me just how significant it is. On this basis I am not going to be the one who does not tell you!

Breathing has proven to be one of the easiest and most effective ways to foster relaxation, build confidence, and direct focus. Breathing oxygenates every cell of your body, from your brain to your vital organs. Without sufficient oxygen your body becomes more susceptible to health problems. In a study published in The Lancet, cardiac patients who took 12 to 14 shallow breaths per minute (six breaths per minute is considered optimal) were more likely to have low levels of blood oxygen, which "may impair skeletal, muscle and metabolic function, and lead to muscle atrophy and exercise intolerance." So you see, every time I struggled to keep going, through lack of oxygen to my muscles and my lungs I quickly became exhausted. Every time my vast efforts sent me purple in the face, every time my muscles ached through sheer exertion, could have been avoided with a) a few basic exercises to improve the way I breathe and b) an awareness of how my breathing affects my ability to work with my horse. Deep diaphragmatic breathing raises levels of blood oxygen thus improving physical fitness and mental performance.

If you are anything like me, you want me someone to give you that magical positional tweak that will revolutionise your riding, well here it is. Get a conscious control of your breathing. Do it early in your training because as you progress and things click into place, you will be looking to refine everything; relax everything;

make it more subtle and strip it back to its heart. As a result you will need to learn to control your breathing whilst in the saddle. Every breath you share with your horse is an authentic cue either to relax or not. Breathing correctly means your chest will expand; your ribcage will lift; your vertebrae will re-align; your muscles will soften; your jaw will relax; your elbows will unlock and your legs will hang long and soft. Breathing correctly means that the oxygen gets to your brain and you are able to think more clearly; communication is calm and responsive.

Breathing it seems is a bit of a lame suggestion in the face of all that you need to do to ride well. Such an insignificant idea barely warrants a try doesn't it? But in my opinion that does not make it any less of a phenomenon but more of one. It is simple and as such should be embraced because 'simplicity is the key to brilliance'. Let's be honest, whenever breathing becomes a chore you are in trouble. "Relax!", "Stop holding your breath!" Whilst these phrases are intended to be helpful, what affect do they really have? When you hit difficulty the first thing to go is the quality of your breathing, perhaps you hold your breath or begin breathing in short, shallow breaths, irregularly. This is very different from your breathing when you are calm, confident, and in control when your breaths are smooth, deep and rhythmic. Mastering the art of breathing will help you deal with the physical changes you need to make. Yes, I know you know how to breathe, but are you really breathing or are you just breathing? Poor posture, anxious thinking, tension and pressure will usually result in breathing patterns which are less-than-ideal and which frequently involves rapid, upper chest breathing only. Conversely anxiety and tension can hinder relaxed breathing coupled with the physical effort you are exerting this can really zap your energy and hinder efficient muscle usage. Having an appreciation of the benefits of 'good' breathing when you ride is a very simple, easy to do, yet hugely positive component to correct posture. Learning to breathe from the diaphragm will compel you to sit up.

The bizarre truth is that learning to control your breathing is not some 10 week course where you need to seek professional help, pay exorbitant fees and work hard to achieve. All you need to do is take a deep breath, put the emphasis on breathing from the diaphragm (or belly) instead of the chest; this produces feelings of being calm and relaxed. Diaphragmatic breathing is the most natural way of breathing. Watch how a very young baby breathes; they will use their diaphragm (belly) with each breath. By relearning to use your diaphragm to reduce the rate and regulate your breathing you will be taking an important first step in promoting relaxation in your riding and your horse's way of going. This slow, relaxed, and deep method of breathing takes a little time to acquire and can be practised at every opportunity, not just in the saddle. What could be more natural than an act that we do some 20,000 times each day? It is a fact that the majority of us take our breathing for granted. Recognise that you are re-educating your breathing mechanism after what has probably been years of misuse. Your breathing technique can create relaxation and rhythm. Isn't this the essence of all things dressage?

Crystal's Tips

- Walk your horse. Inhale and keep your shoulders down, let your stomach expand and get 'fat' while you keep your shoulders down. By doing so, you're lowering your diaphragm and taking in a really deep breath. Exhale, keep your back straight (do not collapse in the saddle), and feel your seat getting heavier in the saddle. It's as simple as that, the better you breathe, the more quickly you'll get relaxation. Do this for about 5 to 10 minutes, practice whilst out on a hack.

- Inhale deeply and slowly through your nose – feel your chest expand top to bottom. Feel your belly push outward as if you were inflating a balloon. Hold for a moment before exhaling – concentrate on feeling calm and patient. Exhale gently through your mouth at a steady rate – be sure to exhale for a beat longer than you inhaled. Feel your belly flatten. Feel the muscles in your arms and shoulders relax while your body melts gently towards the ground. Let your muscles enjoy this moment of relaxation.

- Drop your shoulders and let go. Breathe deep, expand your rib cage to give your heart room and exhale the calm. Inhale. Think of what you want to achieve in a positive light. Exhale. Inhale. We will do a fabulously flowing shoulder-in today. Exhale. The deep breath is actually an act of self-confidence in itself. Taking a deep breath can be used effectively in a lesson, before going into the arena at a show, during any breaks in your schooling or even during a hack. It helps you maintain your composure, control your anxiety, keep your focus, and aids your body in getting the oxygen it needs to operate to its full capacity.

PELVIS AND HIPS

Ok, I need you to be fresh and alert. I need you to really sit up and listen to this section. It is incredibly important. The pelvis and hips are the literal and absolute centre of effort in riding. How many riders would respond with the answer 'hip' when asked 'which is the most important joint in your body for riding?' It is absolutely vital that you understand this and work at ensuring that this region of your body works. Your horse reflects your movement much more than you realise.

Independence

Trainers will usually apply the term independent seat when they are trying to correct a rider who has a dependence on the rein to maintain their balance whilst in the saddle; or as a way of achieving collection; or to pull a horse's head into a so-called 'outline' to give the appearance of him being 'on the bit'. Many riders struggle with letting go of the rein because they simply have no understanding of how the pelvis controls the forward motion of your horse. Acquiring an independent seat takes a great deal of time and dedication. Due to the patience and time required a truly independent seat is a rarity in dressage, when it really should be something for beginners. So, if you have difficulty sitting the canter or your sitting trot is none too smooth; maybe you have trouble sitting deeply or your knees turn out. All of these issues can be resolved from the hip and pelvic area.

Open Your Hips

I heard the phrase 'open your hips' a gazillion times and you know what I did? I opened my legs; I pushed down into the saddle; I lifted my leg away from the saddle to open them. I'd love it if you were thinking, yes that's what I do, that way I feel a little less silly as I felt when it clicked that 'open your hips' means 'open the angle of your hip'. Yeah, that's right … nothing to do with thigh stretching. But open the hip we must do. Understanding what is meant by opening the hip is going to dissolve many issues. Ask yourself this - Where are your hips? Some people automatically think of the point of the hip (that is the bit where the model puts her hand) others think of the point at the outside of the leg. In riding we need to consider the hips' action to know what we need to change about it. So when looking for the hip we are looking for the hip joint, not the hip bone, so we need to delve deep and feel for the movement of the joint, the ball and socket bit.

Align The Hips

Symmetry in your horse's body is an integral part of dressage training. Equally symmetry in the rider's body is an integral part of your training. It is the hips that decide the position of the upper body, in effect if your hips are aligned vertically to the saddle, the upper body will follow that line. If the hip comes behind the vertical you will take a chair position; round your back, your knees will come off the saddle and your legs would slide forward. Likewise if your hips come in front of the vertical (often known as sitting on the fork) your legs and knees would be taken too far back; the upper body would become unsteady and you would easily lose balance.

The ability to rotate the torso is essential for a rider. By this I do not mean fully rotate 360 degrees, obviously, that'd be freaky. I mean to be able to turn the torso left and right. Turning a horse and asking for lateral movements require the rider's torso to be in line with the horse's body. An interesting observation is that if your horse is stiff on one side, typically you, the rider are too. Here we have a 'chicken and egg' situation. What comes first, the rider asymmetry or the horse asymmetry? Every case is different and if you have an asymmetry (which is likely if you are having any straightness issues) you need to decide whether you are the cause or whether your horse is the cause. Either way you will both need to be seen by a professional Physiotherapist to straighten you out. Absolutely no use whatsoever having the Physio to your horse and not getting yourself looked at.

Following

Another one of the most central things I have learnt is to match the movement of my hips and pelvis to the movement of my horse, without any resistance. Moving with my horse's motion not only makes riding more comfortable, but I am sending very clear messages to my horse. Your horse should feel the same freedom in your hips that you feel in his when he's striding out covering the ground. When there is no resistance in our body we move in unity and it is as if we are one, and that's a good feeling, like dancing. To be in unity you want good contact with your horse while allowing the movement of your torso to go with your horse's stride. All dressage movements require you to follow your horse's movement. Often what happens is that you apply your aids, say in the corner and stop following, you effectively block your horse's movement because your brain is applied elsewhere (this is where improving your response times and co-ordination will help) and you have 'forgotten' to go with the movement.

The Psoas Muscles

There are a set of muscles which have direct connections to your abdomen, pelvis and the ability to rotate your thigh - the Psoas muscles. The way they are intricately embroiled around our pelvic region is symbolic of their importance to our riding and ability to absorb the movement of our horse effectively. A contracted Psoas muscle tilts the pelvis forwards and pulls the rider's seat up and out of the forwards flow of movement. This is one of the causes of the incorrect hollow or 'braced' back. Discovering these muscles is an absolute must for any rider with dressage ambition. For those of us who sit all day working at a computer, or driving, our Psoas muscles will inevitably be tight and contracted. If they remain tight and contracted for long enough they will think that this is the norm leaving us with no alternative but to bounce in the saddle from a stiff lower back, 'muscle/movement-memory' runs the show.

It's a being (not doing) position. Before you exercise or at the end of the day, constructive rest changes the whole expression of the central nervous system. There's a lot going on in constructive rest but you're not doing it. You just allow it to happen

Liz Koch

The most important exercises we can do off our horse, to help us on our horse, are those which release tension in the Psoas muscles, which have to be soft and supple to enable you to respond to the movement of your horse. My advice is to set about discovering these muscles for yourself.

Once you have discovered these muscles, but more importantly, once you have released these muscles, you will soften your diaphragm; enable correct breathing; be able to sit on your horse better; calm yourself, and your horse. Your abdominals, inner thighs seem to automatically become toned the moment the Psoas are released and the lower back lengthened. Two weeks is more than enough, and you will feel postural and movement changes 'in the right direction' within the first three days, and to some degree, within the first hour, of practice. And guess what? Tight Psoas muscles require hamstring muscles to over tighten to overcome the forward pull of tight Psoas muscles. It works the other way too: tight hamstrings require Psoas muscles to tighten up. If your hamstrings are tight so will your Psoas muscles be.

Right now, you may have partial (if any) control of your Psoas muscles and they may be 'stuck' tight. Having 'control' means that you tense, relax, and move with your Psoas muscles in a well-coordinated way. What you need is to free and coordinate your Psoas and glutei minimi muscles and the other, central movers and stabilizers of the body for a healthy core (not possible from mere "core strengthening" or "core workouts"). I am not qualified to tell you how, suffice to say that you need a suitably qualified practitioner to help you in this process.

Someone who is qualified to advise about the Psoas Muscle is Liz Koch author of The Psoas Book. She has been investigating, teaching and writing about the psoas for over thirty years. Koch believes that the best release for most people, especially when they are beginning, is what she calls constructive rest, which is a relaxation technique. *Koch states "It's a being (not doing) position. Before you exercise or at the end of the day, constructive rest changes the whole expression of the central nervous system. There's a lot going on in constructive rest but you're not doing it. You just allow it to happen"* I strongly recommend you look her up.. I got really excited when I found Liz because her method of release is the probably the most simple thing you will ever do to aid your ability to position yourself effectively for dressage and simplicity is another of my obsessions.

Crystal's Tips

- **To locate your hip joint.** In a sitting position, either on a chair or in the saddle, use your index finger to follow along the crease of your pants at the top of your leg, move your knee left and right and feel the ball joint movement in the groin area, just move your finger along a little at a time, you will know when you hit the spot, it's a little bit EWW! Now, here's the good bit. Lift and lower your leg (only very small movements) and feel how the hip joint closes and opens. Now feel this on the other side, notice how close together the hips joints are, above the seat bones and towards the front of the pelvis. Fold forward and feel the movement of the joint and lean back to feel how the hip angle opens. So, whenever, you are experiencing the bounce, open the angle of your hips, think about how the ball and socket joint works; sit tall and straight (pricking ears) and allow everything else to fall into place.

- **Experiment by following with your seat.** In the walk, really exaggerate the following movement, rock your hips. You may find your horse becomes irregular in the walk as you push him out of his rhythm. Follow this with a complete stop in the motion of your hips. See the effect it has on your horse. Find the natural balance between pushing with the seat and blocking with the seat. This is where your following seat is correct.

- Your mental walk through the sequence of any movement should always include a check that you are following the movement. So for example: Half halt, inside leg, establish bend, follow movement.

SEAT BONES AND NEUTRAL SPINE

For me the exploration and discovery of how much my seat affects my horse was pretty enlightening and fascinating. There are many different schools of thought and rather incredibly, valid arguments for each, however, in my experience the most effective for the art of dressage requires for 'the seat' to allow distribution of your weight through your seat bones, buttocks and upper thighs; balancing over the centre of the saddle. You 'sit' upright on a vertical pelvis (but not stiffly) and you should be relaxed without slouching; much easier said than done. I have spoken about sitting on a horse. I need you to contemplate the possibility that you do not sit on a horse. Sitting enables you to take all the weight from all of your lower body and have no further use for your legs. This is not the case when riding. You must consider that you are astride your horse, using your seat bones and inner thighs to hold the weight of your upper body, with a little lower leg and absorption of the movement through your ankles.

The term 'three-point-seat' has been around for centuries and it refers to the seat bones and the pubic bone. Rocking on just two-point, under the buttocks leads to instability while sending out endlessly confusing aids; likewise if the rider rounds or convexes the back this may lead to the tail/coccyx being turned under the core/trunk. The very act of sitting compresses the stacking arrangement of the spine and by virtue of gravity it will flatten the lumbar by curling it under and thus reduce the ability to absorb movement effectively. To compensate you will often see riders pushing their stomachs forward and arching the lower back, again not permitting the vertical stack which allows a free and cushioning 'S' shape arrangement for absorption of movement. This is the Neutral Spine. It is my view that, only by ensuring you have full three-point contact with the saddle, can you hope to remain over your horse's centre of balance. But beware, it is through flexibility of the spine that you absorb the movement; a straight back that is rigid is as bad as one that is hollow or collapsed.

The seat bones are said to be in 'neutral' position on straight lines meaning that they are balanced and even and the inside seat bones are engaged on corners.

I say engaged because so often I see riders virtually hanging off the side of their horse when all that is needed is a little more weight to the inside; just a little more pressure and then release.

Crystal's Tips

- Try to think of stretching up when you ride, like, someone has you by the ears from above, stretch up your neck and 'straighten' your spine. (Another oxymoron because the straight spine from a side view actually has a slight 'S' shape, however viewed from the front or back it would need to be straight). Sometimes it is better to think of opening upwards from the waist, lifting the lower rib cage and keeping the navel and sternum projected, the spine will take its own correct alignment from this.

- To experiment with how little seat bone action you need walk your horse on a loose rein in the arena. Do NOT pick up the reins. Ride a circle (10 or 6m) by engaging the inside seat bone first and aligning the hips and shoulders on the circle. Your horse should turn. Keep moving your horse around the arena like this, with constant changes of direction. It is a useful exercise to teach them to respond to your seat and keep you aware of the influence of your seat.

- In the saddle, find your seat bones by bringing the knees up to the pommel and then try to lower the bottom into the deepest part of the seat of the saddle then let the legs drop long down your horse's side. This will initially start you off with the feeling of the seat bones being in the correct part of the saddle.

- Imagine someone just told you that you look like you lost weight, you would draw up, pull in the stomach, smile and say – "oh thank you, do you think so?" This is the 'stretched up' feeling you want in the saddle.

- You may have been told to 'relax the upper body'; what is actually meant by this is allow your upper body to grow taller and expand the torso, thereby releasing the tension in the upper body.

BUTTOCKS

Something no female likes to hear is 'you have heavy buttocks'. But it is something you will wish you had when training for dressage. Tightness in the buttocks emanates down the legs and up the torso and is one of the biggest contributors to balance problems in the saddle. Heavy buttocks will allow your legs and ankles to relax and has a revolutionary effect on your riding. You may have to keep thinking about relaxing that 'glutus maximus' until it comes naturally to you. Oh, and when I say 'heavy buttocks' I do not mean weighty, slouching in the saddle, sitting on the back of the cantle, slopping around in any way shape or form, I am talking of a relaxed or actually, not so tense as to affect your horses way of going, sort of heavy.

Crystal's Tips

- Have you tried Max-Relax? This requires you to exaggerate your tension to a 'ridiculous' level and then release it. So, if you find that you tend to tense your glutus maximus in the saddle try this:

- While on a tolerant horse, inhale and contract your ass muscles so intensely that they turn into hard rocks and you are lifted out of the saddle and your upper body shoots forward. Hold the contraction until you start shaking (or laughing uncontrollably) then totally let the tightness go as you exhale. Let your upper body rock back and picture your legs melting onto your horse. Just really let go. Now get 'normal', that is sit with an appropriate amount of muscle tension and alertness for riding. This now feels quite relaxed compared to the max tension. Remember this feeling it's the one you want when you register that you are tensing. This is the actual relaxed state you are aiming for, 'normal'.

- You can do max-relax in a variety of situations. It will help you to register a specific feeling and a physiological response. Perhaps it is your shoulders that are tense, your arms or your thigh. Your goal is to be able to draw on the normal feeling during times of muscle tension and recreate the 'relaxation' response.

UPPER THIGH

For those of us who were taught to keep the knee away from the saddle, the angle of the upper thigh position can be so engrained that it takes a great deal of effort to rectify. Your thighs should sit softly against the saddle, without tension, so difficult to grasp and so, so difficult to achieve. Often the effort of trying to sit softly creates the tension you are trying to avoid. So many riders have issues relating to what I call 'creepy legs', where the legs 'creep up' and the rider loses the stirrups. Sad to say, any rider that has had a problem for some time with legs that creep up and/or forward are displaying the symptoms of muscle memory which will take some fixing (I'm talking months of concentrated effort). There are two areas to address: the physical and the psychological nature of the problem.

Crystal's Tips

- Muscle memory issues must be addressed at the early stages of your training. Without addressing the tension in your muscles you will not be able to progress through the scales of training.

- Having trained your body to have an 'off' switch, how about letting go of any mental tension which may be building up? Your brain will be releasing tension related signals whether you are conscious of them or not. Riding with a pattern like inner thighs tightening, or heels creeping up, or legs creeping forward causes a constant firing signal to the muscles involved. It creates a very strong 'on' signal to those areas. Teaching your brain to have an 'off' switch by stretching and pausing is a good start.

The best way to start is by stretching the tight areas. Now I know that this is not easy. You have enough to do right? When are you going to find the time to go through a thorough stretching regime? Well I'm sorry to be the one to tell you, but all the time you are spending trying to sit deeper, push the weight into your heels, grip on for dear life is wasted time. Only by putting aside some quality time (around 10 minutes) to go through some stretching exercises, focussed on the muscle groups in the legs, will you see results. Not immediately, but soon.

If you have creepy legs, you have to do the exercises, no ifs or buts; they just have to be done. Another simple method of fixing the improper muscle firing sequence which should be utilised alongside stretching is to pause it. Continuing just strengthens it, so instead of continuing trying to hold the tense position, stop, refocus, get back into position and off we go again. After all, you know when your horse is ready to stretch or needs a break; you have exactly the same need when you are trying to fix an ingrained problem. At first, you may have to pause quite a lot and if you are truly committed to advancing your riding, you may have to spend several rides pausing, your horse may not get his full workout, but the time will be worth it. As long as you are seeing progression and the time between the pausing is getting longer, you can continue, happy in the knowledge that your legs will soon no longer be 'creepy'.

KNEES

The knee, like the thigh, should lie flat on the saddle, should never move from it and no gripping action should occur. This is what Mark calls having a 'floppy knee'. This might be a somewhat tricky concept to grasp but it is intended to bring to you the importance of the lack of action that the knee should take. It is not about the knee being off the saddle and flopping about but ensuring true relaxation in the knee. Gripping with the knees, like balancing through the reins is another strong human instinct and very, very easy to do and when you do so you are pushed out of the saddle. To have the knee 'lie flat on the saddle' means stretching extremely important muscles: the quadriceps group in the upper thigh. Until these muscles have learned to let go, if you try to 'sit up straight' and 'lengthen the legs' you will be doomed to failure and we go into the same scenario as if the pelvis is not vertical. The muscles which are short and unable to let go will pull the thighs up and with them, the knees; if you allow the leg to hang deeper (managing to get the heel under the hip) you will more than likely tend to topple forward. The muscles have to be stretched, if they are contracted you can think about relaxing whilst in the saddle as much as you like but you will still grip.

Crystal's Tips

- Take one session of your training to concentrate on how your knee is working. If it is coming on and off the saddle, focus on keeping it against the saddle without tension. Keep doing this until it becomes a habit.

- Pinching with the knees comes from sitting on your horse like you are sitting on a chair. Mount your horse and adopt the 3 point position – memorise the feeling. Now take weight off the pubic bone and see what happens to your knees. They will pinch.

- It follows therefore, when your knee is pinching you are sitting like you are in a chair and not on the 3-point. Use this as a trigger to make the adjustment.

- Being aware of the way you use your knee when riding can be something you experiment with when taking a relaxed hack. No pressure, just sit on your three point and relax the leg down.

Your knees are designed to move in one direction only, they are not meant to move side to side or rotate like other joints. When we ride, we compress this straight structure against the apex of a round surface, your horse's barrel. This creates a side-to-side stress on the joint that it was not meant to endure, hence the reason why so many riders suffer with knee pain.

CALF AND ANKLES

The term independence can be rightly assigned to describe a rider's ability to use each body part independently of the other. So for example, using the lower leg should not result in a tightening of the thigh or movement in the hip. Each body part is flexible and strong enough to do its job without any compensation in another part of the body. You need to feel like you could unscrew your top half from your bottom half. The ultimate aim is for your seat and thighs down to the knees to lie close to your horse's body. The upper part of your body from the hips upwards and the legs from the knees downwards are entirely independent of the centre and independently moveable. The lower leg is often asked to be 'on the girth'. This means that the toe of the rider's boot is in line with the front edge of the girth;

Crystal's Tips

- Have a go at riding in half-seat. This is where you get off your seat, out of the saddle and find a balance that is more forward over your horse's centre of gravity. It's a very dynamic position and gives the rider a real awareness of how you move with your horse. When you do this you will (should) really feel the way your calf and ankles absorb your movement. There should be no knee grip or flapping of elbows. Concentrate on your rhythm. It's really good fun.

- Sit on your horse and whilst standing take your 3-point position, sit up and hold your hands in 'riding' position. Now move your lower leg backwards and forwards from the knee without moving any other part of your body. It is so easy to do. This is the tiny range of movement you need whilst in motion and clearly demonstrates the 'less is more' principle.

  – Have someone on the ground check your alignment

  – If possible get some mirrors

  – Try not to tip your ankle, keep it level with the toe forward.

legs should be under your body; stirrup leathers vertical; calf angled down towards your horse's hind feet; the heel at the end point of a long stretch in that direction.

We all know the term 'Achilles Heel', often used to describe a deadly weakness in spite of overall strength, which can actually or potentially lead to downfall. The Achilles tendon is one of the longer tendons in your body, from the bones of your heel to your calf muscles. In riding it is the Achilles tendon which allows your ankle to act as a soft and flexible antenna. The stirrup has absolutely no use whatsoever other than somewhere to softly rest your foot.

FEET

Think of your stirrups as snugly fitting slippers, soft and warm and gently supporting your foot. Then, forget about them. Did you know that it is the alignment of your lower back that determines whether your weight 'falls' into your heel. Here's the thing, if your back is hollowed you will not be able to get your weight into your heels correctly no matter how hard you try. This is an essential biomechanical fact! Riders can spend hours trying to stretch their calves, jamming the heels down only to have the legs creep up, seemingly with a mind of their own. They resign themselves to being unable to achieve this most basic principle of a good riding position.

How many riders do you see that point their toes out? Many riders find it difficult to ride with their toes facing forward, instead turning the foot out. When asked to point their toes forward they often respond by using their large leg muscles to twist the whole leg. The ability to hold this position is limited and determined by their endurance level. Instead, try to

Crystal's Tips

- Stand up, feet forward, hip width apart and stick out your bottom, hollowing your back, you should feel the weight transfer to your toes. Now flatten your back, align your hips and relax your shoulders. Did you feel it? The weight transfers to your heels. So, Eureka eh?

- Instead of driving your heel down and pressing on your stirrup, which will cause you to push off the stirrup when rising, (took me ages to stop putting too much weight in my stirrups!) try to imagine tightening the cords in the back of your knee to raise your toes – slightly.

- The positioning of the foot on the stirrup has an immense influence on the position of the lower leg. If you are struggling with the lower leg position, experiment with where you place the foot into the stirrup. I found that by positioning the stirrup a centimetre forward of my usual position it helped me to stop pushing off from the stirrup in the rise at trot, and also helped with heel alignment.

think of your inside ankle bone as parallel to your horse's side and adjust the foot accordingly. It is quite amazing what a difference this makes in enabling you to maintain a correct position. You seem able to subtly adjust your position rather than employing exhaustible leg muscles to hold the leg in place. The foot should be parallel to your horse's side. The heel should be the lowest point of the foot. A secure foot with heels at the lowest point comes from a solid, flat back position and supple, relaxed joints; in particular swinging hips, floppy knees and soft ankles. Your leg weight must fall through the heel in a direction toward your horse's hind foot with your knee slightly bent. In order to achieve heels down you need to be subtle about it and not jam them down; have them level or just below the horizontal. When the leg is long and the heel down, the calf muscle is slightly taught and so can give a clearer, more defined leg aid that your horse has no excuse but to listen to.

"The foot bones connected to the leg bone. The leg bones connected to the knee bone. The knee bones connected to the thigh bone. Doin' the skeleton dance. The thigh bones connected to the hip bone. The hip bones connected to the backbone. The backbones connected to the neck bone. Doin' the skeleton dance". I don't really want you to do the skeleton dance, my point is this … every element of your body is interconnected. Don't assume because your feet are rogue that it's your feet that are the problem. The bottom line is that it could be your head dropping forward, hunching your shoulders and thereby not allowing your lower back to support the flex of the ankle. This is a holistic approach. When you encounter problems, stand back, take an overview of yourself, with the video capabilities of todays phones it's easy to get a friend to video you. Start in the mid-section with pelvis and hips, look at your overall position, and assess every tiny piece of the puzzle, however small. The devil is in the detail.

A note about asymmetry …

… You are having a lesson. Your issue is that your outside shoulder drops and turns to the outside on the right rein. Your trainer explains what is happening and demonstrates how your body position is affecting your horse. You are very clear in your mind what is going wrong and what you need to do to rectify it. It's your turn to show what you have learnt. You put yourself into position and off you go onto the right rein. You start off with the shoulders in alignment with your horse but before you have turned half a circle the shoulder has dropped and is tuned in the wrong way, exactly as you had before the instruction. You do it wrong and the trainer has to remind you.

Procedural memory, like riding a bike

Are you not trying? Are you an idiot? Of course not, you are perfectly normal and have reacted exactly just as 85% of riders do. Why? Because of muscle memory. Most of us have come across this term at some point in our training, but it is not a memory stored in the muscles, of course, but memories stored in your brain. If you're practising your riding skills over and over again, the idea is that you'll continue to improve, after all 'practice makes perfect' right? The more you do something, you build up what is known as 'procedural memory' and your brain can fairly quickly learn to instruct your muscles to carry out its instructions. That's great isn't it? All we have to do is regularly repeat. Like learning to ride a bike, you can become very good at something through repetition, but in exactly the same way it can make you weak at that very same thing. Your muscle memory can and often does play against you if you've constantly been practising something the wrong way.

Muscle memory doesn't have the ability to judge whether you are riding well or not so if you practise sitting crookedly (unknowingly) for hours on end you're going to be really good at making those same mistakes over and over again. When you repeat faults again and again, you build a muscle memory firing sequence with all those mistakes built in. That makes them really hard to overcome and is the very reason why some rider faults plague us. I liken it to that incredibly irritating matter of rolled up sleeves that fall down. You are training, you are getting hot so, up go the sleeves. You feel the sleeves creeping down your arms but it is ok because they're only just past the elbow. Before you know it you are getting hotter but you don't know why. Then you realise you're sleeves are down and you have to push them back up. This is exactly the same as your muscle memory. It happens in your subconscious, without your knowledge and before you know it your hip has collapsed and you are sitting crooked. It takes something in your conscious state to have you make the correction to your position.

Discovering my muscle memory issues explained to me why, after many years of riding, I had not progressed. I was not using my hands, legs and body the way I thought I was using them. Because of this, I practised the training techniques over and over but made no real improvement. The key to building good muscle memories is to focus on the quality of the work, not the quantity and here is that old saying again, 'practice makes perfect', well, no it doesn't actually, only 'perfect' practice makes perfect. You may have heard, probably from Malcolm Gladwell's book Outliers, that 10,000 hours is the magic number to make you an expert. It's likely that this is the case when you practice well, but if you spend those 10,000 hours practising ineffectively you will build procedural memory in your muscles over and over again and guess what? You get really good at repeating your mistakes. Most of us don't want to be expert anyway, competent will do. So it is not going to take 10,000 hours for you to eradicate those irksome rider faults that sneak in and out of your riding.

As always, be patient. In time you won't have to consciously tell your body 'keep your hands closed' the body just knows how to do it, largely because neurons communicate with the muscles and say, 'close hands'. Using the muscles in a positive way thus becomes an unconscious process in exactly the same way as the original issue became ingrained. The muscles grow accustomed to certain types of movement; extremely important in training for dressage. The more often you do a certain activity, the more likely you are to do it as needed, when needed. You want your muscle memory to reflect the correct way to do things, not

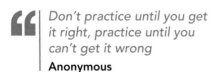
Don't practice until you get it right, practice until you can't get it wrong
Anonymous

the incorrect way. Now take a minute to equate this to your horse and his way of going. He too may have muscle memory issues, it is your job to find them and help your horse to release and become supple enough to accomplish the manege exercises with ease.

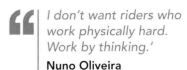

I don't want riders who work physically hard. Work by thinking.'
Nuno Oliveira

We have established that it is generally accepted that good muscle memory is best cultivated when the same activities are practised over and over again, with any corrections of form that are needed. It appears however, that despite this

SUMMARY CHECKLIST TO FIND THE BEAUTY IN YOUR RIDING POSITION:

Look up and through the ears of your horse, prick your own ears and smile

Shoulders low and relaxed

Feel your arms falling naturally by your sides and relax them from the shoulder

Give only from the elbows

Back of hand in line with forearm, creating slightly rounded wrists, hands gently closed, fingers relaxed, bent thumb

Regulate your breathing, lift lower ribcage

Open the angle of your hips, match your horses movement with your hips and pelvis

Find your seat bones and neutral spine

Relax your buttocks

Thighs and knees resting gently against the saddle

Legs loose, falling naturally and vertically, never sticking to your horse or squeezing

Pause your tension signals

Floppy knees

Calves 'off' your horse

Absorbing, limber ankles, no tension

Foot simply resting in the stirrups on the first third of the foot

Weight falling into heels naturally, not under pressure, toes forward

practice, attitude can interfere with muscle memory; nerves can lead to clenched or tight muscles that can't quite perform as they would if you weren't thinking about it and self-doubt about your abilities to perform may also affect muscle memory. The 'lack of confidence' factor can over-ride any positive strides achieved in rectifying muscle memory faults by regular practice. The classical master Nuno Oliveira said, *'I don't want riders who work physically hard. Work by thinking.'* When you consider that even the training of your muscles is actually down to the training of your brain to work your muscles. The way you approach your riding can overcome even this very strong rudimentary instinct. Surely you can begin to appreciate the 80% strategy - 20% activity approach to your training.

There you have it, a top to toe analysis, some exercises and tips to help you achieve the ultimately effective riding position. I feel sure you will already have identified plenty to be working on and in the final few chapters we will begin to put your newly acquired knowledge of how your mind and body works into practice. But just in case you are so desperate to get to the 'How To Ride Your Horse' bits that you haven't fully taken in the top to toe analysis come back to this chapter and go through it again. You may get more from the top to toe analysis the second time you read it.

Stretch your body, Stretch your mind, Stretch your limits. Let's do it!

Stretch your body. Stretch your mind. Stretch your limits

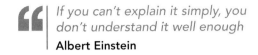

> *If you can't explain it simply, you don't understand it well enough*
> **Albert Einstein**

DO – The Simple Things Matter

By now you will be crystal clear about why you are doing this, what it is you want to do and whether your fitness matches your aspirations, found some clarity in your thinking and you will have identified any body parts that may (or may not) be working correctly.

Now we come to the actual riding element of this self-help system, where the goal is to enable you to put into place the basic requirements to enable you to train your horse and for you, as a team, to come together and be as one.

How your horse feels on a given day depends on your riding skills. This statement is true, but there are other factors that will have an impact on your ride. It will depend on your horse's temperament, when he was last worked, any muscle soreness, the type of tack you use, his feeding regime, the time of day and many more influences and believe me, the very simple things can matter. Your ride starts in the car on the way to the stables, continues in the stable and then as you climb aboard. Getting your mindset right is so important. If you are stressed in traffic, running late and hurry and hustle your horse as you groom and tack up, you will create tension before you even reach the arena and your horse will not be

Physical ability can only get you so far, before that it comes down to attitude

relaxed and even though you apply the correct aids you don't get the response you were expecting; there can be many reasons why.

Physical ability can only get you so far but before that it comes down to attitude. Great riders have a mind-set that is so established, it creates a hugely powerful incentive to adopt certain behaviours or choices that are critical to their training success. No matter what has gone before, a great rider will have the foresight to put everything aside for the ride. In this context I refer to mind-set as a set of assumptions and methods that are ingrained in the way that they go about their work, each and every day. Great riders are shrewd, skilled, progressive, genuine, clever, sensitive, sympathetic, scholarly; acting purposefully in everything they do. It is all about small steps and building blocks. As the old colonial phrase goes, 'slowly slowly catchee monkey' or in other words, the slow and patient approach to any problem with careful thought is often better than rushing in.

The shrewd rider

is realistic in their goals and expectations. They are insightful enough to know that there is no point in 'over-facing' yourself (to steal a jumping phrase). Set small achievable goals that make a pyramid to your 'big picture'.

The skilled rider

lives on a small number of good steps and builds on them. Forget about the really bad things; it is only inexperience that makes you think mostly about the bad things. Put them behind you, dust yourself down and try again.

The progressive rider

knows that success comes one ride at a time. Ensure with each ride that you build upon the best bits of the last one. Start today where you finished yesterday. Make progression a goal and don't get 'stuck in a rut'. When problems arise, address them constructively. Try not to react emotionally.

The genuine rider

embraces negative critique and failure. Failure is not the end but the beginning, be thankful for the information it brings, train yourself to learn its lesson, be accepting that you are potentially giving your horse a problem. Face this fact and make amends.

The clever rider

is consistent and correct. This means they are ready to work through 'the boring stuff' and put much effort into the very basics to be able to one day ask for the more challenging work, only to find that their horse is more than capable. Why? Because the groundwork is established, their horse's way of going is correct; horse and rider can now build on firm foundations.

The sensitive rider

appreciates his horse's mental state, how his horse thinks and adjusts communication accordingly. Only by proving your ability to be your horse's guide will he confidently trust you. You will have to work diligently to earn his trust. Those riders who appreciate that their horse is another living, breathing being that has the grace to allow a rider on his back, are those whose sensitivity show through in their riding – be mindful of this at all times.

The sympathetic rider

understands that there are no short cuts and no-one can do it for you. You are building a partnership so that you can 'dance' together and if you are not prepared to work hard simply don't bother. The amount of success you have as a rider directly relates to the amount of appropriately guided effort you put into it. Play the long game, don't look for instant gratification.

The scholarly rider

enjoys the process. There is no final destination when it comes to dressage; it is a lifetime of learning, accept this and enjoy the journey. Relish the idea that you have a great deal to learn and the more you learn the more you will realise that you do not know.

Crystal Says

Let's help you find your way ...

FEELING THE BASICS

It really does help to recognise the influence we have with our seat as early as we can in our dressage careers, only then can we begin to appreciate how very generous our horses are for allowing us to ride them at all and how we owe it to them to try to be 'at one' with them for this honour. How many riders are able to feel the movement of their horse's hind leg through their seat and really understand what is happening underneath them? There are lots of reasons why we should but I guess that's something else we are not taught as a beginner.

IN THE WALK...

Do you recognise which hind leg is stepping under you?

Do you ever even think about it when you ride?

Are you able to give alternate leg aids and activate the correct leg?

If you were to close your eyes could you call out which leg is stepping under?

As your horse steps through and onto his back foot his hip lifts and pushes one side of your seat bone forward and up and your hip drops when the hoof is off the ground. In the walk, each seat bone alternately goes forward-up-back-down. This is often described as a backward pedalling bicycle sensation. If you can feel this that's great, but in my experience too few riders have grasped this critical skill. Why not work with a friend and ask them to call out 'now' each time the inside hind hoof is on the ground? Feel what is happening with your seat as you do this.

Perfecting the whole movement while seated on a chair (off your horse) goes a long way to making it clear to your conscious mind and the neural pathways to the muscles involved which makes it easier for you to transfer that feeling to your riding.

Walking Seat-bones:

- Sit on a hard stool or bench, back not leaning against anything, thighs parallel to the ground, feet hip width apart and feet planted on the ground.

- Round and arch your back several times to find the place where you are neither arched or rounded and your seat bones are pointing straight down (Neutral Spine).

- From this position, slowly begin to slide your left seat bone forward and back, just a millimetre or two, about 10 times and pause. Repeat on the right then rest a while.

- Same position - this time slowly lift your left seat bone, raise it and lower it. Close your eyes and notice the movement or tension in your ribs, sensations in your collarbones, neck and feet. Perhaps you are leaning in either direction; perhaps your back is arching or bending.

- Now, having established the forwards and back and up and down movements, very slowly slide your left seat-bone forward–up–back–down just as you do in the backward cycling motion of the walk on horseback. Repeat on the right then get up and have a walk around.

- Are you able to do this smoothly? Where do you get stuck? Can you feel the sensation of the movement everywhere in your body? Perhaps you could exaggerate the movement in your upper body and then bring it back with more tone into your torso so your pelvis makes the movement but your head and shoulders are relatively still (like when you are riding).

- Try alternating between sliding each seat-bone forward-up-back-down, as if you were riding a walking horse. So, left seat bone forward-up-back-down, right seat bone forward-up-back-down. If you were on a horse, would he feel resistance or would he feel you absorbing and going with his motion, evenly weighted on each seat bone?

- Whilst walking your horse follow his movement with your seat and then stop. Notice the difference between you allowing the forward motion and you blocking it with the stop. That way when you feel the block you can adjust your following movement accordingly.

Do you need to visually check your diagonal when rising?

Is it automatic to you and always correct?

Can you feel when you take the wrong diagonal?

Do you think about the hind legs as you go into trot so that you are absolutely clear which diagonal you are rising on?

This is another area where as a beginner we tend to think about the front of the horse to help us achieve the correct diagonal. We are told that as the outside shoulder comes back you should sit and if it is incorrect, sit for one beat and rise again. This method of teaching encourages you to look down at the shoulder to check your diagonal rising is correct and essentially gives you no guidance whatsoever on how to feel it. It encourages you to a) move your focus to the front of your horse and b) puts you in front of the movement by throwing you off balance. It is the easy way to do it and if you have been taught this way you should feel a little cheated. Your trainer has simply robbed you of the ability to feel what is happening underneath you through your seat. How many of you begin rising and then check that you have the right diagonal? And, how much better would it be for you to feel what is happening underneath you and select the correct time to begin rising?

This is a clear demonstration of why you need to be able to feel the footfalls in walk, through your seat. Just to re-iterate. On the right rein, tune into the left (outside) seat bone. As your horse's back dips on the left, this is the sit phase. When your horse's back

Crystal's Tips

Have a go at this …

- At the walk, feel your hips lifting and say 'now' every time your 'outside' hip lifts up.

- Then move up to a few strides of sitting trot.

- In order to feel the correct diagonal, feel when your 'outside' hip lifts up.

- Every time your outside hip comes up, say 'up'.

- Begin rising (posting) on the word up.

- Hey presto, you are rising on the correct diagonal.

(and therefore, the left seat bone) rises on the left, is the rise phase. It may take some concentration and coordination at first, but with practice it will become second nature. Feeling your diagonals instead of looking will raise your horsemanship to a higher level and help to develop your sense of feel of how your horse moves. Eventually you will know when you are on the wrong diagonal because it will feel out of balance.

Crystal's Tip

- The whole topic of feeling footfalls, from walk to trot to canter can be fun with a friend, particularly if you struggle alone, you will benefit from having a friend in the arena with you who can confirm that you are indeed feeling things correctly.

IN THE CANTER ...

Do you know which leg is doing what through your seat?

Do you time your canter depart aids in conjunction with your horse's footfalls?

Do you time your aid to coincide with the exact moment that the outside hind is about to come to the ground?

The canter is a three beat pace, where in the canter to the right, for example, the footfall is as follows:

- left (outside) hind
- simultaneous diagonal pair - left (outside) fore and right (inside) hind
- right (inside) fore
- moment of suspension with all four feet in the air
- the next stride begins

Most horses will understand your canter aid whenever it is given and be willing to depart into canter as soon as they can. But if you're having trouble, if your horse is sensitive, if you truly want your horse to progress through the levels or if you're riding a horse that has been trained to a higher level than you, you will want to give your aids at the right moment.

So, here's the reason you need to feel the hind legs through your seat bones in the trot. It is the outside hind leg that begins the canter depart and when in trot, it is when the outside hind leg is coming through that you need to give the aid for canter depart.

If you have worked on recognising when you are on the correct diagonal this would be during the sit phase of the trot. However, as you do not ask for the canter depart directly from rising trot and will need to be in sitting trot for at least a couple of strides before you ask for canter you really must work on being able to feel when the outside hind is coming through in the trot (more specifically as its getting ready to push off). This is when your horse's hip lowers on that side.

I hope that I have demonstrated that feeling your horse's hind legs through your seat in walk will aid your transition to trot. Feeling your horse's hind legs through your seat in trot will aid your canter depart. These are exercises that you can incorporate into your training on a daily basis. Once you have mastered the feelings of walk, trot and canter through your seat, spend a few minutes each session honing these skills. When you progress through the levels and begin lateral work, collected work, tempi changes, pirouettes etc., in fact whatever level you work at, however experienced you are, whatever your level of ability, if your goal is to work in harmony with your horse you must achieve and maintain this basic skill.

Simplicity is the key to success. It is the simple things that matter and simply being able to feel your horse's gait under you is not difficult, complicated or arduous. It is simple. So why not take a few minutes each session to master this skill.

> *Start by doing what's necessary; then do what's possible; and suddenly you are doing the impossible*
>
> **Francis of Assisi**

DO – Your Horse's Way of Going

You will have come a long way if you have followed this program as it was intended. We now need to turn to your horse and look at his way of going.

There are a number of essential elements to the way your horse works which are fundamental to your dressage success. They are forwardness, rhythm and relaxation, tempo and straightness. Without a clear understanding of their importance and a basic knowledge of how to achieve them you simply will not be able to perform a basic training test and unquestionably you will not be able to progress the levels.

FORWARD

If there were a one size fits all solution and I could just pinpoint one thing that would assist every rider it would be my very favourite 'F' word – Forwardness. Having your horse forward quite simply erases 80% of all issues. Fact! (bold I know, but I need you to understand this). Ensuring your horse is forward really is the first port of call for many, many issues. Without the urge to go forward from the leg, to be a forward thinker, the half-halt, which is the cornerstone of balance, engagement and preparation for just about everything is just not effective. How can you 'check' something that is not advancing?

Forward has nothing to do with speed

Forward has nothing to do with speed, if you are used to a short striding, slow gait having your horse forward might feel a little 'too fast' at first but a forward thinking horse which is attentive, active and has energy that can be channelled is a much better prospect than one that needs frequent reminders and is 'behind the leg' (a term which is used to describe a horse that requires constant reminders from the leg to go forward).

I have had a succession of riding instructors that have screamed "more leg", "put your leg on" to the point where I had convinced myself that I did not have strong enough legs for the job. Imagine then what a relief it was to me discover that the better way is 'Leg On, then immediately off', if you do not get the response, 'on again and immediately off', no response? 'Tap with the schooling whip, behind the leg as you apply the leg aid and immediately off'. When you get the response you want, keep the leg OFF. Not only a relief but how beautifully it works. I do not have to clamp my legs onto my horse to keep it going, even when asking for my horse to move away from the leg laterally it is 'on and off', not constant pressure. My horse is sharp to the aids and I am less tired. Seriously, throughout this journey I have been continually surprised that my gargantuan efforts have been hindering my progress and less is, undeniably more.

For your horse to be forward you have to be effective with your aids. Consider just how effective you really are. Does your horse immediately respond? Are your aids crisp, clear and true? Or are you having a numbing effect on your horse? There is nothing wrong with being a 'lazy rider' if what you are referring to is that you want your horse to do most of the work. There are a number of issues associated with why your horse might not be 'in front of the leg'. It's all about 'blocking' the energy flow. We need to continually appraise whether we are doing something that may have blocked a free forward motion. Here I have listed some common ways riders restrict forward motion that can help you evaluate whether the problem is with you or your horse.

Are You Blocking With Your Seat?

Your following seat must move with your horse's motion in a rhythmical way in order to allow your horse to move forward. If you say 'go' with your leg aids but your seat does not immediately follow the forward swing of your horse's hips as he picks up a hind foot, you will restrict forward motion – guaranteed. Are any of these rider symptoms familiar?

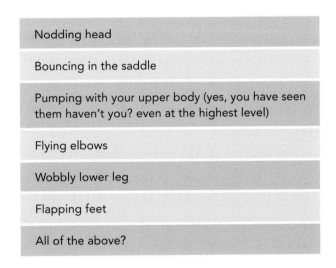

Nodding head

Bouncing in the saddle

Pumping with your upper body (yes, you have seen them haven't you? even at the highest level)

Flying elbows

Wobbly lower leg

Flapping feet

All of the above?

These are common symptoms of tense hips that are not correctly following your horse's motion. You may be cheating by collapsing at the belly button to absorb the motion or pumping with your upper body at the canter. Ok, now you have recognised yourself bouncing, pumping, head bobbing, elbowing and leg flapping, do you think you should take up what comes naturally - *kick boxing?* Or is there something we can do about it? Well, you will need to work on thinking tall and elegant and transferring the rocking to the pelvis instead of the upper body. Do the pricking ears exercise in the Head and Neck section of Chapter 7 – Discover – The Beauty In Your Body.   You need to identify the issue and refer back to Chapter 7 for a potential solution. The object is to follow your horse's motion by opening and closing the hip angle whilst maintaining a steady, relaxed upper body.

Are You Blocking With Your Leg?

If you use constant leg pressure to hold your position on your horse, or squeeze and hold with your legs, some horses feel this as a restriction of movement rather than as an encouragement to go forward. Your horse may have been trained to stop from the leg. Sensitive horses may try to run away from it. Either way, not correct. Riders can tend to grip with the knee and thigh or turn their toes out and hang on with their calves. If you try to enforce these incorrect leg aids with a touch of the whip, your horse may kick out, buck or balk as a way of saying, "Not fair! mixed message!" A squeeze and release with the leg urges your horse forward rhythmically. A softly supporting leg can steady a flighty horse. A gripping leg can often restrict forward movement.

Are You Blocking With The Hand?

This is such an obvious block, saying 'go' with the leg and 'stop' at the same time with the rein. That will just confuse your horse. Less obvious is the more advanced rider who has tension in their hands. This will feel backwards to your horse and he will respond accordingly. That's if you have a generous horse, if not you could get a reaction you may not wish for. Do not allow tight fingers, tense forearms or locked elbows, your horse's forward motion will be blocked. Your ultimate aim is to feel like your horse is taking you forward without too much effort.

RHYTHM AND RELAXATION

Every horse has his own cadence, or 'inner music'. When trying to find it, it is easy to confuse slowness and laziness, or speed and impulsion. Too fast and your horse will stiffen, the stride shortens and loses relaxation. Too slow and the rhythm is compromised and laboured. It's all about the rhythm and relaxation; because without it the gait can't be wonderful and you will not have cadence. Cadence can be explained as the rhythmical movements of your horse's stride. Your horse is said to be expressing cadence when he appears to be moving in harmony with you and with well-marked regularity, impulsion and balance.

I like to think of cadence with a musical connotation. Think of the metronome used to produce regular, metrical beats (clicks), used by musicians to keep a steady tempo, it is used to work on issues of irregular timing, your horses paces should be a regular four beats for walk, two beats for trot and three beats for canter, regularity of the paces as stated earlier, being a primary objective.

So what exactly is rhythm? It is described as a 'regular recurring motion' in the dictionary. The regular recurring motion that a horse maintains in all his gaits and paces is a major factor to your dressage success. Rhythm and relaxation go hand-in-hand because it is nearly impossible to have rhythm without relaxation. When we talk of relaxation of the horse we refer to the horse's mental state: calmness, without anxiety or nervousness and the horse's physical state: the absence of muscular tension other than the contraction needed for optimal carriage, strength, range and fluency of movement. Relaxation of the horse's emotional and physical state goes hand in hand.

Rhythm contributes significantly to work at the upper levels. Preparing your horse mentally and physically is vital to his future as a dressage horse. No exercise or movement can be considered good if the rhythm falters. Developing rhythm and relaxation will gradually strengthen your horse to be able to do the movements that will require great physical strength later in the training.   It is this looseness that enables your horse to work free from tension or constraint. Suppleness plays an equally important role in your horse's relaxation. A horse that is stiff or rigid in any part of his body will not be capable of utilising his body effectively, thus resulting in irregular gaits, unwillingness and a general displeasure in his work. The first major test of relaxation is to find out if your horse will stretch his head and neck forwards and down in all three gaits. In order to work effectively on rhythm and relaxation you need to work on your own balance and not rely on the reins or gripping with the legs for support. Look for a pace that feels light and flowing, supple, smooth, easy.

Imagine your horse ambling along in walk, jogging instead of trotting, stumbling through a test constantly breaking the three beat canter. Not often do you see all of these faults in one horse but sure as night follows day you will experience these faults, at least to some extent, if you have not focussed your training on rhythm.

Because in this small, rather oddly spelled word (should be ritham, right?) you have wrapped up a whole host of skills you and your horse must master; energy, even tempo, clear and regular paces, balance, contact and so on. If you consider that impurities or irregularities in the rhythm, tempo and stride length are serious flaws in your horse's ability to perform you can begin to appreciate that not only should you begin the training process by focussing on rhythm, but you should remain focussed on rhythm throughout your riding career.

The walk is the gait that is most prone to impurities. You can have considerable influence on the way your horse walks which means that you can induce faults too. So, if you over ride the walk and push your horse into a faster, bigger walk than he is capable of, he will fall onto the forehand and tighten his back. Likewise if you attempt to collect more than your horse is capable of, his back will tighten and the walk will become irregular. Consider your 'free walk on a long rein'. Your horse needs to show a clear, pure, four-beat walk and most likely is able to – as long as the rider is not touching reins, then immediately the rider picks up the reins, the horse responds with unequal strides. This happens as a result of the rider using too much rein; not enough leg support and usually too heavy a seat. Go figure. Relaxing more and reducing the demands will in most cases restore the clear four beat rhythm.

The safest way out of a jig jog trot is to start the working trot afresh, establish the rhythm and relaxation and when the hind legs have started thrusting and the back has started swinging again, the walk will most likely be improved as well. The important point I would like to make here is, as with many, many other issues, you will not be able to regulate your horse's paces without a good forward thrust, so first of all check that you have a forward thinking and willing horse, otherwise you will not have anything to work with.

The majority of young horses, and horses that are being retrained, need to be reminded periodically not to slack off the forward propulsion. Left to their own devices they will gradually fade after a few strides with good effort and that means the power with which their hind legs propel decreases, the gait loses its intensity and becomes dull. The result? The horse's back stops swinging and the trot deteriorates into a jog, loses its gymnastic value and the horse's musculature development over his haunches, back and top line is hindered. This coupled with the potential issue of losing forwardness on the corners if the horse is not strong enough or trying to avoid the flexing of his joints and you may have to go back to basics and that means rhythm.

Here's some food for thought, like your heartbeat is the 'rhythm of life' so rhythm is to your horse's gymnastic development, without it – not going to happen.

TEMPO

Many people use the words rhythm and tempo interchangeably so it is not surprising that you may be confused between the two. They do not mean the same thing. Regularity of the rhythm in riding refers to the even spacing between each step in a stride of walk, trot or canter. Rhythm is the regular defined beat pattern in which the hooves fall. So you may see irregular rhythm – (for example in a 4 beat canter or a 'stuttery' walk). Rhythm is not the speed with which your horse's hooves touch the ground. That is tempo.

Tempo is the speed of your horse, so, depending on how fast you want to go you can adjust the rate of repetition of the rhythm. So you may lose the regularity of the beat, and therefore lose the rhythm whilst keeping a steady tempo; but you may also speed up or slow down in which case you lose the tempo (they are inextricably linked). You would, without doubt, feel a loss of rhythm if your horse's feet get quicker, but it is the tempo that is being lost and having a resultant effect on the rhythm. Another way of looking at it is in terms of energy. A horse galloping on the flat might develop a good rhythm with a (very) fast tempo. A horse plodding along barely moving in trot can still be rhythmical but the tempo would be slow.

Most untrained horses assume that the leg aid means 'speed up', so they increase the tempo as soon as the rider asks, thus losing rhythm. This is perfectly normal and acceptable at lower level training, however, as you move up the levels it is up to you to clarify with your horse that the leg aid means 'put more effort into your work, but keep your tempo'. This is achieved using an effective half-halt. So it is through systematic training and with the establishment of rhythm that you can begin to teach your horse to adjust the tempo, adjust the stride length and adjust his energy levels independently of each other.

Loss of impulsion and slowing of the tempo often happens because keeping the impulsion and tempo require more strength from your horse. Pay really close attention to the regularity of the tempo, stride length and energy level throughout all exercises, patterns, and movements in order to develop the purity of the gaits to the highest level and to develop your horse's strength and suppleness to his fullest potential in the process. You have to be progressive in your training. Your horse will respond with little and often. It will take six weeks for him to build the muscle power and stamina required to be able to efficiently execute new and demanding exercises. Too much too soon could result in injury.

There are a number of times that you will often see horses varying the tempo of the gait by speeding up or slowing down. Nine times out of ten this will be due to them trying to avoid the more difficult flex of the haunches or thrusting with full ability. Most frequently this can be seen in the form of slowing on the approach to the short side and speeding up again at the beginning of the long side; essentially, slowing on the corners.

Another common tempo irregularity occurs during transitions, say walk to trot, the walk gets quicker or in canter to trot, the canter gets slower. Likewise, making transitions into and out of lateral movements is where you will most likely see your horse speed up or slow down, but for the most part losing tempo. In every single case, the unwanted change of tempo is caused by a loss of balance and a lack of ability to flex. Before you go pushing your horse through the corners, transitions and laterals, think about exercises to develop his ability to flex and bend. Check whether your horse is capable of the flex and only when you are sure he is, can you concentrate your work on the actual tempo and improvement of his pace.

STRAIGHTNESS

Straightness is generally defined as a horse that 'tracks true'. That is, when the hind leg follows in the track of the fore leg on the same side. Each hind leg should bear equal weight. Straightness in your work (and therefore, your horse) is critical from the very beginning of your training. There are no ifs or buts though; you should always, always look to yourself when you have straightness problems. All too often I hear riders objecting because their horse 'tries to get away with this' or 'is lazy' when in fact the horse is doing exactly as the rider has been asking, only the rider didn't realise it. With straightness issues you need to take a step back and observe what is happening.

A Case In Point - No. 1:

A rider was riding a beautiful relaxed, long and low walk on the left rein, when she switched to the right rein her horse contracted, quickened the pace, jogged a little and would not stretch down. Mark was asked to take a look at the horse because the rider felt that the horse was crooked and something was wrong. There was something wrong. He asked the rider to relax everything down the inside of her body on the change of direction to the right rein thus ensuring she was sitting evenly in the saddle. The horse stayed relaxed and the problem was sorted. It was that easy. The horse was not crooked, but going quarters in and tight because the rider was asking for quarters in, she had a slightly collapsed hip (very, very slight, but this was a very sensitive advanced horse) and as soon as she addressed the imbalance the horse responded appropriately, as indeed it had been doing all along.

A Case In Point - No. 2

Mark was asked to ride a horse that kept pulling up in the right canter. He found that the horse wanted to bend his neck excessively and not bend his body on the circle and as a result couldn't sustain the canter. With a little experimentation with the hand and leg aids he found that if he supported the horse with the outside rein and positioned the outside leg to ask for a bigger bend than the horse was used to he would canter a circle all day long!
All he had to do was position the horse 'straight' on the circle correctly.

Being straight on a circle is one of those horsey idioms that, in my view, are just designed to confuse. Keeping the neck straight on a circle means following the line of the curve of the circle, so we say that the horse is 'nicely straight' if he has executed a good bend and the hind legs are following the line of the front legs. What it does not mean is that your horse's neck should be 'straight' as a board. Many horses are what we call 'one-sided'. They favour a 'good rein' just like we favour left or right handedness. If your horse is good on one rein but not the other, it could be because you have trained him to be that way. Here's what to check out if you are having straightness issues:

Inconsistent, or un-level rein contact

Posture issues, rider one-sidedness, get a friend to check you out

Tension in your body (thigh, shoulders, arms)

You are not riding your horse forward enough. So many times I have been told that a horse doesn't like schooling or is lazy in the school, only to find that the rider is blocking their horse's forward motion by leaning forward and giving the aids to collect or slow down, only for the horse to free up and move readily when the rider stops blocking the movement.

> **Bridle or bit fitting issues.** Problems in the mouth will inevitably show through lack of straightness as your horse compensates.

> **Confusing aids.** Be very clear in your aids. Talk yourself through them as you do them, just so that you know you are not confusing your horse and asking him to move laterally.

> **You are restricting your horse's natural head nod.** One of my favourite sayings 'still hands move'. Yes, they move with the motion of your horse's head.

> **Dentistry.** Get your horse's teeth checked and don't be afraid to get a second opinion. I have lost count of the number of times I have miraculously cured a problem by advising a second check by a dental technician.

This dressage thing, it's all about you helping your horse to be the best he can be. If you feel that your horse is not straight, look to yourself. I guarantee that you will be inadvertently asking for the unevenness or you will have trained your horse to be uneven, which is sad, but true. The irony is that in order to rectify issues and train straightness into our horses we almost never 'go straight'. You need to strive for and maintain suppleness in your horse so that he is flexible enough to use his muscles on both sides of the body evenly. In Chapter 12 we look at 'Suppling The Horse' and it is by concentrating on these exercises that we teach ourselves and our horses to be supple enough to 'track true'. Your horse's needs are vast and complicated, he may think all he needs is feeding, but all equestrians know how ridiculous this statement is. You have far wider ranging responsibilities and his physical development is one of them. So concentrate on ensuring that both you and your horse are straight in the way you move.

Forward, rhythm and relaxation, tempo, straightness. Understand what these words mean; assess yourself and your horse for each element; make adjustments and corrections where you need to; set yourself goals to get them mastered; work on them in every training session; incorporate them into everything you do.

Crystal Says

Now you can begin to influence your horse …

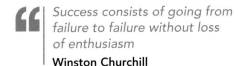

*Success consists of going from
failure to failure without loss
of enthusiasm*
Winston Churchill

DO – Influencing Your Horse

All exercises must be executed properly otherwise they do not improve your horse at all and are of no value. There is a difference between just riding and actually influencing, in a positive way, your horse's way of going.

Of course, everything we do influences our horse's way of going and it is worth taking on board my primary message to you 'If you get the right response when you ask correctly, it surely follows that if you get the wrong response, you may not be asking correctly'.

We have already looked at a myriad of aspects of your position and how it affects your ability to be a skilful rider. With your newly acquired knowledge we should now begin to look at how you can develop into being more than a just passenger. Only when you have progressed and have a truly independent seat will you be actually capable of positively influencing your horse. Nevertheless, this is what we should all aim towards; having the necessary skills to train our horses correctly, evaluating them, getting to know their personalities, their little nuances and quirks, recognising and supporting their needs in the arena, developing their body and mind in a progressive way.

With the key elements of your horse's way of going understood; forwardness, rhythm and relaxation, tempo and straightness, I understand why it might feel like forever before a rider reaches the point where they can train a horse. The important point to remember is that whatever it is that you are working on, you must never compromise forwardness, rhythm and relaxation, tempo and straightness. As we move on to the section of this training program that more specifically, requires you and your horse as a combination to come together, the four key elements must remain the staple of your training and be revisited every time you ride.

In this chapter we focus on the things that will aid your ability to influence your horse. Indeed, in my experience, without them you will forever remain a passenger with the accompanying frustrations. What are these things?

Your ability to recognise imbalances in your horse and stay in balance whilst riding

To establish and maintain a useful contact and therefore a connection with your horse

The use of the half-halt

Understanding the outside rein and its effect

Working in a long and low frame

The power of transitions

How shapes and accuracy enable your ability to influence

Walking and its potential to shape your riding

And finally, the square halt and why it is so important.

Develop your abilities in these areas and you will soon be on your way to becoming extremely competent rider.

STAYING IN BALANCE

Understanding just how much your body and position affects your horse's way of going is the key. We hear a lot of talk about achieving balance for both horse and rider. Perception of imbalance really depends on the discipline you choose. We choose dressage, which means that certain behaviours and characteristics of how a horse moves in the field are not required or desired under saddle. That is not to say that there's something wrong, just that we don't want any imbalances in the arena.

Take a look at the list to see if you can identify any issues that may indicate some type of imbalance that needs addressing in your training.

Perception of imbalance depends on the discipline you choose

RECOGNISING IMBALANCES

Ability to do something on one side but not the other

Turning circles and corners like a boat instead of a train

Falling in on the inside shoulder on a circle and corners

Falling out over the outside shoulder on a circle

Hard in the mouth and or holding on to the bit on one side

Heavy in the hand and leaning on the reins

Unable or unwilling to stretch the neck

Incorrect strike off in canter or going disunited in canter

Moving laterally when not asked

Unable to execute a square halt

Speeding up, jogging, shortened steps

Irregular rhythm or bridle lameness

Head tilting or shaking

Grinding teeth

Tongue hangs out of mouth

Swishing tail

Every horse bends more easily to one side than to the other, this is known as 'lateral asymmetry' but if your horse is excessively so you need to address the problem with exercises to help stretch out the contracted side and contract the strung out side. He may have a 'horizontal imbalance' (commonly known as on-the-forehand) which is the natural way for a horse to carry himself. It is only when he carries a rider that we need to train him to carry more weight behind. Or he may have a 'diagonal imbalance' when the point of the horses weight is off-centre and he goes 'out through the shoulder'. Finally a 'vertical imbalance' is when the horse does not give an upright impression but one of leaning (especially in canter) – like a barrel racer.

Sometimes I feel a little ridiculous when I think of some of the things I say "oh, my horse's tail is swishing, that must be an imbalance"! Really? Yes, really. In the pursuit of perfection every detail counts and whilst I am happy for my horse to swish her tail, if she does it excessively she is trying to tell me something.

Ensuring you are 'in balance' with your horse whilst he is constantly changing centre of gravity takes time to learn. The trick is relaxation of the lower body, which includes those jolly buttocks, whilst the upper body remains upright, supporting itself. You need to feel like you could unscrew yourself from the waist and separate the two parts. The aids given with the legs should absolutely not affect the upper body. You can achieve this by noticing whether you are collapsing in the upper body with the effort of giving the leg aids. If this is the case, re-establish your position and try again until your leg is able to go 'on' and 'off' independently of the rest of your body. Once again, you could be putting in too much effort! It will take much practise, but just being aware of when you have achieved it and more importantly, when it is all going wrong will help you get there.

A USEFUL CONTACT

The dictionary definition of connect is to join, link or fasten together, to unite or to establish a sympathetic harmonious relationship. In these days of social media we think of connecting as adding friends, or linking profiles, networking, whichever way you look at it making a connection with someone or something is about you putting in some effort so that you can come together. When that something is a horse and you are thinking about dressage riding, developing a clear, non-verbal language with your horse means making a connection and is where your dressage journey begins.

The most frequent answer to the question 'what are you struggling with' is something that is absolutely vital to your dressage success and that is 'contact'. Without a useful contact you will be unable to communicate with your horse; you will be unable to 'engage in any type of conversation' or convey any message effectively. It's a really widespread problem. It is what is known as a back to front problem and can escalate and create more issues such as gait changes (working to medium trot) becoming difficult, movements are downhill instead of uphill and your horse begins to lean or back off the leg. Too much focus on the reins makes you a 'front to back' rider. Swapping your thinking will solve a multitude of problems. Establishing and maintaining a contact, making a connection, being above the bit, getting behind the bit, head tilting, head wobbling/shaking, strong contact, soft contact; there are a myriad of issues, so for those of you that need help let's explore a little further and see if we can get you on track.

Unfortunately, expecting something to be difficult to achieve can often become a self-fulfilling prophecy. So, in order for you to begin the process of achieving a 'usable contact' with your horse you must decide for yourself that it can be done. That is, decide yes, you may face obstacles that will be challenging for you, you may have to sort out a few issues, most likely with your riding but sometimes with your horse (teeth, back), sometimes tack issues (saddle, bit), but get your mind set right and choose to believe that you and your horse are not only willing but are more than capable of working in an outline; with a contact; on the aids; on the bit, call it what you will.

Why Do You Ride Your Horse 'On The Bit'?

This primary question, which all aspiring dressage riders should at least consider, is often overlooked and misunderstood. Why? Well, physically a 'round outline' is the silhouette shape that is seen from hocks to nose and comes about when you ride your horse forward into a good contact. It is the flexion of the hind limbs that has a direct effect upon your horse's ability to flex his jaw and lower his nose. The flexed limbs create the energy which travels from behind, over the back, through the neck, and into your hands at which point it is required to be recycled back to the hind legs. This will only occur if you have a 'useable contact'. If you have no contact, the energy will seep out through the front and not be recycled, creating balance and rhythm issues. With the hind limbs stepping further forward the transference of weight will take place from the forehand to the quarters thus the forehand will 'lighten'.

The horse that is 'round' and 'on the bit' is adjusted to take the riders weight easily to comfortably carry you and use his body effortlessly. When we climb aboard a horse he has to brace his back muscles, so it is important that we make it as easy as we can for him and build the muscles he needs correctly. A horse which is not able to carry the rider properly will become tense and uncomfortable and likely to be evasive and disobedient. It follows then, that to carry you comfortably, your horse needs your help. Why would you not want to do this for your friend?

Unfortunately, 'on the bit' is a much used and abused term. The phrase is somewhat misunderstood and many riders are confused as to the correct meaning. In my view a better terminology is 'on the aids', because what we are describing is a horse that is listening, willingly going forward, using the energy being created from your forward thrusting aid; submitting to these aids and comfortable in the mouth and as such is accepting of the bit. The rider does not 'put the horse on the bit'. The horse is said to be 'on the bit' (a term that so inadequately describes what you are really putting your effort into training towards) when he seeks and accepts the contact with the bit as offered by you, the rider. You become connected.

How Do I Know I Have A Connection?

It helps to know when you have successfully connected and have a good contact and it is relatively easy to recognise. When you and your horse are connected through the contact he becomes a lot more comfortable to sit on because his back is relaxed. The trot and canter gaits feel more bouncy because your horse's back is swinging. You feel in control and like you can work though transitions, smoothly and promptly; your horse will be 'in front of the leg' (so will not need continual reminders from you to keep going); he will feel light and obedient. This is because he is 'on the aids', willing, submissive and ready for your instructions without resistance in the mouth or body. Believe me, once you have felt what it feels like to have your horse connected a) you know about it and b) you will not want to ride him any other way.

There are things that you do when you ride that have become automatic to you, like asking your horse to walk on from a standstill and putting your foot in the stirrup to mount, with practice and repetition everything you do can become second nature. Dressage is not some sort of magical, mystical jiggery-pokery, the simpler you keep things the more straightforward it all becomes. However, when we talk about lightness in the contact there is good lightness and bad lightness. Bad lightness is when you feel lightness in the rein but actually what you have is NO contact, either a looped rein or worse a 'wishy-washy' rein that will constantly prod your horse and may even be causing him discomfort in the mouth and certainly will be creating inconsistencies in your communication. Good lightness is the stable 'feel' in your hands, no pulling, not strong or downward deadness but still a good feel in the hands.

Just one more point about false lightness. If you use a severe bit which your horse does not wish to touch, he will not be 'on the bit' he will be afraid to touch it and you will have a false lightness.

Where Do I Start?

To initiate contact with your horse, you must shorten the reins (no pulling). Many riders believe that shortened reins means pulling reins, nothing could be further from the truth. You should aim to achieve a 'useful rein length' that allows a secure feel of the bit in your horse's mouth. It should be steady, which is where it gets tricky; take up the rein contact, and keep it steady, but you must allow and follow your horses head movement. All too often I see riders who worry that their hands are not steady enough so they stiffen their arms in an effort to keep their hands still thinking that a steady contact is keeping everything still. It is not, you must 'allow' or your rein will actually be on-off, on-off or loop/straight, loop/straight with the movement of your horses head.

So, what does 'still hands' really mean? Still hands start at the shoulders. The shoulders should be 'back and down'. Elbows should rest against the torso. Now is the time for you to make a conscious recognition that your horse is moving. Therefore, if you are in harmony with your horse, you will be moving too. The horse moves his head forward and back in walk. In trot the head and neck move up and down and in canter the head moves up and down as well as forward and back. In all of these paces it is best if the rider 'allows' this movement with the hands. It takes time and practice to synchronise one's hands to the movement of your horse, but once mastered it is a technique which becomes second nature, like mounting.

Next, invite your horse to reach forward into the rein contact. This can be thought of as a 'handshake' with your horse, where your horse comes to meet you. Just like when you reach forward to shake someone's hand, they reach forward, and you make contact! Ask your horse forward from your legs and seat. Create a millimetre of space for your horse to reach into (from a giving elbow movement – don't drop the reins or let them through your hands). You should feel your horse surge forward with a lifted back. This is an indication that you are on the right track.

When you first get on and walk on a loose rein it is reasonable for your horse to be allowed to do whatever he wants with his body. However, when you pick up the contact you need to give a number of aids to help him become round.

He can be relatively long and low, but he should always be round when working. You should begin by adjusting your seat. Place the legs in the correct position; align your pelvis, shoulders and seat-bones. These are the three key ingredients to begin making a good connection with your horse.

KEY INGREDIENTS...

1. First of all your horse needs to be (you guessed it!) forward, so send him forward with your legs and following seat. Remember you are creating energy and recycling it so it is the energy creation that comes first - leg before rein. It is essential that your horse goes forward immediately when you close your legs. Without the forward thrust your horse will arch his neck and make a shape as a result of your hand actions but he won't be connected. So, first check that your horse is in front of your leg by asking for a really forward trot.

2. Next, use the bend to encourage the flex of the hind legs. Inside leg on girth, outside leg behind the girth, seat bone weight to the inside (watch out for that vertical imbalance though, not too much)

3. Third and final ingredient is your outside rein. This is the rein that controls the speed; the rein that controls the bend; the rein that stops 'too much' happening. It should remain constant and your horse should learn to trust it. I've heard it called 'the indirect rein of opposition' but frankly I can't be bothered to even fathom what this might mean. You ask your horse to flex "in" at the jaw, by moving the bit in his mouth with vibrations of the ring finger. Be sure you only use one rein (the outside rein) to move the bit, the inside rein should remain stable. Fiddling with the bit and/or seesawing on your horse's mouth with your hands will pull the jaw 'in' but without the forward trust, there's no true connection from back to front, it will give you a false head set and your horse will hollow his back. Once you learn how to get a true connection, you won't feel the need to fiddle with the bit.

To find out where you are in this process, there are two movements that are both found in the Novice Tests. The first is where the horse and rider are asked to allow a stretch on a circle and the second is the give and retake of the rein.

Testing The Connection – Stretchy Circle

If your horse is round from his hocks to his poll it is a natural progression for him to want to seek the bit when you allow some space with the reins. Hence the stretchy circle is a good test of whether you have your horse 'on the aids'. If your horse doesn't eagerly stretch forward, down, and out when you relax your fingers as you start the stretchy circle, it's a sign that you are not 100% connected. However, be aware that if you simply let the reins out, even if you have started with a good connection, your horse is probably going to fall on the forehand and rush forward. That's because he can't balance himself. As you're allowing your horse to stretch, please do not lean forward, stay upright and tighten your stomach muscles to assist your horse in maintaining the same tempo and resist rushing. Gently open the fingers and allow your horse to take the rein forward and keep in mind that nothing else changes. The only difference is a stretch. Think forward, rhythm and relaxation, tempo and straightness.

Testing The Connection – Give And Re-take

Another test of whether your horse is working in 'an outline' and in 'self-carriage' is where you show a clear release of the reins for a couple of strides. So, if you've successfully connected your horse you ought to be able to put a loop in the reins for a couple strides and nothing should change. That is, he should not bend to the outside he should not put his head in the air, he should not speed up, he should not lose his balance, everything remains the same because you have him connected with your seat and legs.

Again, the technique you employ to test this will obviously have an effect. The judge, in a test, is looking for your horse to maintain the head carriage. If you throw the reins forward your horse may think you are a rodeo rider and react accordingly. Firstly ensure you release both reins, releasing just one rein is a bit of a cheat. We are testing your connection here so try to be honest with yourself. What you need to do is gently allow the hand forward from the elbow about two inches towards the bit (not up the neck). You need to ensure sufficient release of the contact smoothly over a few strides and back again. Finally, ensure that you put a loop into the rein. In a test situation you will not get a good mark if the judge doesn't see the release of the contact.

Try both tests to help you establish where you are and assess the work you need to do to begin making a true connection with your horse. If you don't feel like you are there, experiment with the forwardness, bending aids and outside rein and adjust each aid individually until you get the recipe right, then do the tests again to see if your horse will take the bit forward better.

A Word Of Caution

It is worth noting that the novice or untrained horse (whatever the age) needs time to develop strength and flexibility to accomplish the desired 'roundness.' It's important that every time you take a walk break, you should give a loose rein and let your horse adopt any frame he wants so that he can relax his muscles. The length of time you ask your horse to work 'on the bit' depends on the individual horse. Always consider his age, fitness, and temperament. Clearly, if you do too much and make your horse sore because he's using his muscles differently, you're not only going to have a sore horse, but also a horse that becomes quirky and resistant. So the trick with anything you do with a horse is to bring him up to the limit, and then take the pressure off. As soon as your horse shows signs of resistance because he's either physically or mentally tired, back off. Build up day by day.

Maintaining The Outline

Using the connecting aids will set up the right conditions for your horse to accept the contact and make a connection. Likewise you will use the same aids to maintain the outline and correct any balance issues. Sit up tall and utilise your lower back and abdominals to keep your torso upright. If you go limp or collapse your mid-section, you will find that your horse starts leaning on your hand, because he loses self-carriage in his efforts to rebalance where you have put him out of balance, especially if you collapse forward. If you align your shoulders, seat bones, and heels in a vertical line, you will feel that your horse will regain his balance and therefore, his self-carriage.

The main obstruction to connection with your horse is stiffness. Your horse must be free of all stiffness in his body in order for the energy to flow and not leak out anywhere. Your riding position has a mammoth impact on his ability to bend and flex without any energy blockages. Many riders don't realise they have trouble sitting the trot because they have not made a correct contact. No matter how good a rider you are, it's nearly impossible to sit on a back that's stiff and hollow. The key to making both you and your horse more comfortable in sitting trot is to ensure that you have made contact and are engaging in conversation with your horse through your reins.

Contact can always be improved, like communication can always be improved. It develops with the goal of softness, lightness, gentleness and effectiveness of the touch. Good rein contact makes a happy horse and taking all of the above into account, only with soft shoulders, arms, elbows and hands will you achieve a good contact.

INSIDE LEG TO OUTSIDE HAND

Do you fully understand the essential concept of inside leg to outside rein and have the ability to apply it in your training? No? Well this does not surprise me. One of the most perplexing, most difficult concepts in riding is the use of the outside rein to turn a horse. It goes against everything that is hard-wired into our psyche. Most riders, without access to proper instruction, turn their horse like a bicycle. They pull on the inside rein and push the outside rein forward and why not? Surely to turn anything you need to show the direction in which you wish to go? No. In riding dressage you need to discover the supremacy of the outside rein.

The number one rule when employing this way of working is that hands must be even and level at all times. You use inside leg to outside hand, but it is not the use of the outside rein that you should think about. It's about how you apply the inside leg and seat bone. You are looking to encourage your horse to 'fill' the outside rein, not apply more pressure on that rein. The rein contact should be even and the inside leg encourages your horse to put more weight to the outside; inside seat bone also encourages the weight shift whilst the outside rein is merely there to catch this weight shift. The outside rein 'fills' – the inside rein 'softens'. Take a glance down, the outside rein should be firmly 'in play', it will be having a limiting effect, preventing your horse from drifting out over the shoulder and controlling the tempo. When the above occurs correctly, we say you can feel the connection between inside leg and outside hand.

DEVELOPING THE HALF HALT

The horse's natural stance is on the forehand, with his weight over the front of the legs. Your job as the rider is to re-establish your horse's centre of balance and move it further back so that he can carry you comfortably. This balance can only be achieved if you have engaged the most powerful part of your horse which is, of course, the hindquarters. The way we do this is by using the half-halt.

Now I subscribe to what I believe to be the Carl Hester school of thought that the half-halt is a very personally developed aid which differs for every horse/rider combination, is therefore, unique so being crystal clear about how to apply the aids is not easy. So let's say as a very simplified and generic description for the half-halt might be – close the legs to ask for more forward energy and close the fingers on the reins to block that energy and then release. The block ensures that your horse does not run away or drop down onto his forehand but rounds his back, lifts the forehand and steps under himself from behind.

Picture a horse. Now circle the two areas of the horse where energy can escape; the front and the back. The front circle coils clockwise up through your legs, over the wither, down the horse's face, down under the horse's forelegs and back up through the sole of your boot. The hind circle spirals anti-clockwise, comes up through your boots, over the horse's quarters, down under the horse's hind legs and back up through the sole of your boots. In the half-halt, you are aiming to get these two circles closer together.

When your horse is 'on the forehand' energy trails out of the hind end

If you have no contact or are not using the half-halt, the energy will leak out of the front of your horse.

If your horse is not forward, you simply are not creating any energy so forwardness will always be your starting point.

Firstly you should bear in mind that all of the following happens in a fraction of a second and you need to be very, very subtle.

1. The Leg Element of the half-halt.

Close your legs gently and momentarily, asking for forwardness.

2. The Seat Element of the half-halt.

Tilt your pelvis forward (anteriorly) while keeping your lower back flat and straight; your crotch or pubic arc presses forward towards the pommel.

3. The Hand Element of the half-halt.

Your fingers should be relaxed when holding the reins ordinarily, closed but relaxed – now, in the half-halt, close your ring finger on the outside hand a little more.

As your horse feels your resisting hand he should back off the bit slightly.

Instantly reward by relaxing the ring finger.

Remember to be steady in the hand. The goal is to train your horse to expect a request from you (change of rein, transition, change of bend). Developing communication with your horse through half-halts will assist any balance issues enormously. So for me the half-halt is a combination of seat/hand/leg co-ordination, which tells your horse, "I'm going to ask you something different" and it asks your horse to check his pace and go forward (stop and go all at once) thereby helping to transfer his weight to his hindquarters.

Be sure not to pull back in the half-halt, the closing of the fingers is a 'block' to send the energy asked for by the leg back to the hind-legs. If you pull your horse's back will hollow. However you execute the half-halt it must be with finesse and subtleness and the aids should be applied for only a few steps. Prolonged pressure will not give you the desired result, so as your horse responds, back off, soften the rein and then go again.

What is the desired result? You are looking for the hindquarters to be under your horse's centre of effort with the back soft and light shoulders, thus enabling the forelegs greater freedom of movement.

Here's what to do. Always look to the end result, try to feel your way through, try not to be too mechanical about applying the half-halt, play with the pressure until it is achieving the desired result. Experiment and feel your way, too much hand and your horse will back off the forward impulsion, too much leg and he will shoot forward, you will know when you have it. You will feel the containment (or rather flow) of the energy coming up and over the back. However you execute the half-halt it must be with finesse and subtlety and the aids should be applied for only a few steps. Hold in your memory at all times that absolutely nothing about the half-halt is supposed to slow the forward motion; it should just check it and engage the quarters. The leg and seat aids encourage forward, whilst the hand resists (not pulls) so you are creating more energy in order for you to check it and rebalance your horse. If you employ a resisting hand and do not give more encouragement forward you would simply be checking the forward movement that you already had and would not get the effect you are aiming for with the half halt.

The half halt is not a slowing aid. In dressage it is utilised to a) let your horse know that you are going to ask him to do something different and create the energy to do it and b) rebalance your horse and ask for more engagement.

Once you have experienced it, believe me, you will want to be sure that you always use it, because without the ability to recycle the energy you will not feel good about your riding. Think of the half-halt as a balancing aid. The half-halt is a very important influence in making your horse obedient, balanced and 'up' in his way of going. Yet becoming skilled in the half-halt is oh, so difficult.

WORKING IN A LONG AND LOW FRAME

If you are not aware of the benefits of working your horse in a long and low frame, I'm here to tell you about them. When I refer to long and low, I am making a clear distinction between long, deep and round – low, deep and round – and long and low. Because throughout my journey of discovery I was working a young horse (or if you are just starting out in dressage) the majority of my work was done in a long and low frame with the poll never coming above the level of the withers until the last ten minutes of each session. This enabled me to relax my horse, balance and engage the hind quarters because working in this frame your horse takes long even breaths, calming him and putting him in a good frame of mind to work. Your horse's back relaxes and the strides lengthen making greater use of the legs and hind quarters. By stretching out their spine in a long and low frame, they loosen up their muscles which releases calming endorphins and helps them move in a more relaxed and elastic way. This is particularly important in the hind legs which are their 'main motor' and impulsion force. Once they are loose and working at full capacity, through a relaxed spine, your horse's movement, impulsion and expression improve.

Horses must carry a riders' weight on their spine, so it follows that a well-muscled, strong back is essential to their willingness to work. A supple, strong and relaxed back will give your horse a better attitude. With regular work like this your horse's 'top line' of musculature will improve; a rounder, more muscled neck, and a round and more muscled rump.

How is this achieved? Allow your horse to walk on a long rein and when you take up the contact, take it slowly, maintaining soft, following hands on a longer rein than you usually school with. Feel the flexibility through your elbows and feel the contact. Your horse should keep his head and neck below the line of the wither. Once you have established a good stretch on a long rein with a contact you should vibrate the outside rein in order to ask your horse a little lower before the transition into trot and continue to vibrate throughout the transitional strides. Once up into trot cease the vibrations.

It is worth defining what I mean by vibrate here, because this vibration of the rein can be overused and predictably becomes more of a 'jab' or a 'shake' of the rein. For me it is literally a small, rapid and brief movement of the ring finger – a 'quiver' or a 'pulse'. You should have a go at how you are going to vibrate the rein when dismounted, because do not disregard the fact that those vibrations are going directly to your horse's mouth. You need to be subtle about it.

Some horses won't be able to sustain the frame for more than a few strides to begin with because their balance and strength won't be there yet. Often a horse will dive heavily onto the forehand and begin to trip or shuffle. Usually horses like this will need a few sessions over a couple of days before they can be convinced to maintain the trot in a stretching frame. This is because this stretching is a bit like you trying to touch your toes when you get out of bed in the morning. He may offer a little more each stride, until the stride becomes rhythmic and he is able to push his nose out and down. Do not force anything.

You may need to open the rein a little. i.e. take your hands out away from your horses neck (no more than an inch each side to encourage the contact forward. Ensure the trot is forward (this is essential) and immediately off the leg. Keep your hands low, use your fingers to squeeze and release.

Ideally your horse will drop his head for a stride or two and travel with a round frame. You need to maintain a contact but do not hold your horse together. If all is well he will offer to stretch down but you must give and react quickly enough to ensure that your horse is rewarded for his efforts. You should do this until your horse is happily taking the contact forward from walk to trot. Then you can gradually reduce the amount of vibrations you do until it is simply a half-halt before the transition.

Try to be smooth with the way you vibrate through your fingers so as not to upset your horse's mouth. Remember, you are communicating with him through the rein. Try not to shout. If you get a bit wobbly in your seat it's because you are relying on your hands for balance. This is bad but not bad in the urban sense of the word (i.e. good) but it is another good reason to work your horse long and low; to improve your own balance and reduce dependence upon your hands. You will definitely know if you have got it. Your horse's back will lift up to your seat. This lifting sensation is unmistakeable and exactly as described, sensational. Finally, you should be able to work your horse in a long and low frame in all gaits, walk, trot and canter with no loss of roundness throughout transitions.

THE POWER OF TRANSITIONS

In dressage, transitions are the most marked and commented upon part of the test. You are judged on the quality of your transitions and they are as important, if not more so, as your horse's way of going. After all, they are at the beginning and end of every movement you execute so in your hierarchy of 'getting things right' transitions should be right up there.

The classical masters taught that *all training* occurs in transitions and I wholly concur with this. For me, if forward is the 'one size fits all' solution to assist riders in identifying issues with their horse's way of going, and I could pinpoint one thing that would actually improve your horse's way of going, it would be transitions. Incorporating countless transitions into your work will benefit you and your horse in many, many ways.

THE BENEFITS OF TRANSITIONS

Building the hind end muscles

Developing better balance

Maintaining rhythm

Teaching horses to be 'hot off the leg'

Paradoxically – relaxing your horse

Getting your horse supple

Maintaining suppleness in your horse

Aiding obedience

Teaching collection

Teaching extension

Ensuring lightness

Winning marks in your test

Developing harmony

Helping the development of the 'top line' muscles

Engaging the hind quarters

Executing a square halt

Keeping your horse attentive

Developing accuracy

Check that you are in a 'back to front' mind-set and begin the use of the transitions to start your horse's engine. Put a great deal of effort into your transitions, do them well, do lots of them, never accept a sloppy transition. You must have forward impulsion in your upward transitions and you must use your seat and legs in the downward transitions.

Hundreds of perfectly practiced transitions will have a huge benefit to your riding and your horse's way of going. With transitions your horse will find his own balance. But my point is not that there are lots of types of transitions, it is that you really do have to do hundreds of them, so never think that you have done 'too many' transitions. Keep going, even when you have perfected the essential element, which is to preserve balance and maintain rhythm.

The Upward Transition

Transitions are another area of your riding where your enormous efforts may be hindering you. The worst thing you can do in a transition is make too many changes to your position. In an ideal world you should concentrate on maintaining your position, contact and rhythm throughout your transitions. There is no feeling on earth (in my opinion!) like riding a good transition, (except maybe a sensational half-halt). Really think about your transitions and how you execute them.

In the walk to trot transition, when you ask your horse to trot, you should feel your horse respond easily to the leg aid by engaging his hind, accepting your seat by lifting his back and continuing to step under his belly towards the hand and up into trot. If your horse keeps his neck round (his nose can be slightly in front of the vertical) as discussed in the section about contact, the energy created will flow. Please don't be discouraged if you can't get it right immediately. Instead, practise the 'flow' at every opportunity and soon enough, you'll notice that your horse is not getting stuck in his transitions. If he is, then as always, take him back to rhythm and relaxation before you begin to try again but I need to re-iterate the 'don't change anything' message. If you have a good, active free flowing walk, when you ask for the trot, do not adjust your rein contact, body position, leg position or balance in any way. Before every transition you will need to half-halt. This will not only signal to your horse that you wish to make a change but will engage the hindquarters. So just to recap, you use a combination of co-ordinated seat, hand and leg aids in the half-halt.

The Canter Depart

The trot to canter transition is the one that the majority of new dressage riders struggle with. Even when the depart is established there is often a lot of room for improvement. The issue is often with riders leaning forward thereby pushing their horse down onto the forehand and making it impossible for their horse to step up cleanly. These riders may also have the tendency to let go of the contact which allows their horse to drop onto the forehand as a result of the lack of support by the rider. Tell yourself that you're stepping 'Up' into the canter, not forward into the canter. Think 'Up, Up, Up' with your upper body, hands, and leg. Do not push with the leg like your horse is a tube of toothpaste or he will behave like one and rush out in a big splurge. Scoop your horse up under you with the leg. If you are really struggling, lean back and 'look to the skies' when you ask. This temporary measure will really help you communicate the 'Up' message; you can tone it down once you and your horse get the idea.

It is so easy for me to say 'relax', but that is what you must do. If you can't relax your legs and have them entirely independent of your upper body, you should get help to learn how. In my experience the canter depart is a very, very common problem for riders. Those who have the problem seem to think that everyone else can canter perfectly well and they are the only ones struggling. The first thing to note is that it is almost certainly the rider that is creating the issues and recognising this is a huge step to correcting the problem. As with walk to trot, change nothing, just give the aids and sit. You will have established a good rhythmical and forward trot so from this simply hold your position and canter.

The Downward Transition

There is something I need you to know about downward transitions which may perplex you. I apologise in advance for this, particularly as I am an advocate of keeping things so simple. Here goes: It is important at all times to think of the 'downward' transition as 'upwards'. I see many riders allowing their horses to 'flop' or 'fall' into the downward transition. Some horses fall heavily to the forehand and then eventually change gaits, others simply like to quit and put very little effort into supporting their weight from the hind end. Ideally, the energy should be maintained with the same fluidity from say, canter to trot or trot to walk. Think about your upward transitions and how you ask for them, half-halt, leg, following seat and hands. Do exactly the same on the downward transition but with a resisting hand.

You must ask your horse to keep forward so that the hind end drops and powers. Indeed you may need to use a little more leg in the downward transitional strides to encourage your horse forward. Timing is important and when you practice or are training your young horse, don't be discouraged if your horse will not make the transition and continues to canter if you are asking for trot, simply persist with the forward encouragement of the seat and leg, but resist with the hand. That is, block with the hand (not a pull back) simply stop allowing with the hand and eventually, your horse will respond with a forward transition that is fluid and energetic.

You should always be looking up and to where you are going in the downward transition. So often you see riders looking down and burying their horses into the hole they create in the manege. Likewise you should ensure that in your mind set you are a 'back to front rider' concentrating all your efforts on engaging the hind legs, not focussing on the front end and ensuring you have a useful contact.

So, how do you recognise a 'less than perfect' transition? Well, your horse will hollow his back, his head will come up, his weight will be shifted to the forehand; you will feel a loss of rhythm and energy. It will not feel seamless. This may be because you have not prepared properly for the transition, or you may be leaning forward or back; your rein aid may be too strong (pulling). You may not have prepared the preceding gait sufficiently well. As with most things in dressage, 'good begets good'. If the canter is on the forehand, so the transition to trot will be, and so on.

Crystal's Tip

- A good way to practice transitions, whether they are up or down is to count the number of strides you do at each pace before the change, so do eight of walk and then eight of trot. You will know the exact moment you want the transition so can be very precise with your aids, but more importantly you can assess your horse's reaction. This exercise can also facilitate your accuracy.

Developing Variation in the Strides

What is variation? Everyone knows that there are three recognised basic gaits in dressage – walk, trot and canter. But we also have variations within these gaits – medium, free, collected and extended walk; working, medium, collected and extended trot and canter.

You need a holistic approach to teaching your horse variations because, whilst the lengthening and shortening of your horse's steps is important, this element (the length of the steps) is only important in relation to the overall outline or frame; elevation of the steps; raising of the forehand and neck and lowering of the croup. All these elements are thoroughly interconnected. This is an important point for you to understand, because too many people send the front legs flicking out without engagement of the hind quarters. The way you approach the training will set you up for success. Do not set out to merely lengthen the steps when teaching working to medium trot, you should work on lengthening the frame; encouraging more power from behind which will produce a raised forehand.

Developing your horse's ability to vary the gaits relies on your ability to do your transitions well. This in turn relies on your ability to recognise the absolute purity of the footfall within each gait as well as consistent tempo and regularity of the rhythm at all times, especially throughout the transition. When executing your transitions, concentrate on maintaining tempo, relaxation and rhythm, these should not falter. Be aware of the frame you are looking to achieve in each of the variations of the pace. If you are going from working trot to medium, half-halt before the transition and create increased power, allow with the hand after the half-halt so that your horse's frame can lengthen (along with the steps). Think about encouraging the hindquarters, look up to where you are headed and take your eye OFF the front of your horse.

To help your horse achieve and maintain self-carriage try riding him 'on and back' by asking him for a few lengthened strides before asking him to come back to his working pace and repeating it several times in a session (more transitions). To set up, you need to half-halt, and create some energy in your horse's engine.

To balance you both, ride a ten metre circle, come off the circle onto the straight (diagonal or long side), half-halt again and give a little from the elbows whilst encouraging your horse forward with the leg. Just a few strides will do as a start and cease all aids once you have asked. Think about easing out the bigger steps and give your horse time to develop and build up his muscles and balance. Fluency and suppleness over the back are very important. If you get a few strides, half-halt again, sit up and continue the working trot (the back phase).

If your horse runs, ride a 10m circle to rebalance him

If your horse steps become irregular, you have asked too much too soon

If you get no reaction you have not set up correctly in order to create sufficient energy for the (gradual) release

If your horse hollows and stiffens in the back you have used too much hand or insufficient give in the reins.

If your horse goes wide behind you are potentially behind the movement and putting excessive pressure on his loins.

Build up the number of steps you allow. Think of a pressure cooker. If you fully open the valve on a pressure cooker the pressure will be released in one almighty blast and upset everything. If you ease the valve open gently you will get a steady stream of steam. Oh, and remember the building block of every exercise – rhythm. One other thing, we are not aiming at 'flicking toes' here, we are looking to lengthen your horse's strides. That means all four legs.

Slowing the Canter

Swap the words 'slow canter' for 'unhurried canter' and we understand each other. One thing that holds its elusiveness for countless riders longer than any other is the ability to effectively control the canter. Many, many times Mark is asked "how do you get your horse to slow down the canter?" It is a very, very common dilemma. Of course instinct says 'you don't want him slow, you want him forward' which is absolutely right and so easy to say, but if I take myself back to the early days of my training one of my many issues was getting and sustaining a controlled and relaxed canter. Just couldn't do it, simple as. I also know that you will never be able to encourage your horse forward in the canter until you have control and in order to have control, you have to slow the canter. It's a case of, which comes first - Chicken or Egg? Well, the first consideration is the horse itself.

Your horse must be strong to lift his entire weight off the outside hind in the canter and carry you at the same time. Just think about this please. We often assume that a horse can walk, trot and canter, "why won't he do it how I want it?" If it is a young horse or one being re-trained there could be a strength issue. Your horse's entire weight, plus you off the outside hind leg, an extraordinary feat, don't you think? So, if you're horse is experiencing difficulty maintaining balance and a quiet tempo in the canter, he may not be physically capable at this time. He will only be able to maintain a quiet tempo if he has natural athletic ability or the rider is skilful and does not interfere with the balance. Also, if you are retraining an older horse, it will take time to build the physique that your horse needs to carry your weight with ease and therefore steadily.

Of course, the other major issue is that many riders don't ride well enough to give clear aids. If the rider's seat, legs and hands are not correct, the communication cannot be clear. To your horse, it's chaotic and he may have learned to put up with the chaos and thus tune you out and that means one thing – he'll ignore your aids when you think you are giving them. Before you can begin to control the tempo of the canter there must be relaxation in your horse both mentally and physically. A horse that rushes isn't relaxed. Your horse must be supple and swinging through his back. He must have clear acceptance of the bit and the aids. Once you have these elements, you're on the right path.

Because the hindquarters provide the impulsion for a horse's movement, we want to actually use the hindquarters to control, or slow, your horse's forward thrust.

It is your horse's ability to carry more weight on his haunches and not to run on his forehand that needs development and understanding.

To aid your horse's balance, concentrate on keeping his neck straight at the base, in front of the shoulders and the rest of the body will follow. Practise this thoroughly in the walk and trot, in straight lines and on circles. Include many transitions and changes of rein in walk and trot and suppling exercises before you try the canter. You should genuinely feel improvement in the rhythm and tempo of the trot before you attempt to slow the canter. This is because you are working to help your horse carry more weight behind and balance himself; as the trot improves so will his ability to steady the canter.

HERE ARE SOME CONSIDERATIONS ...

Does your horse ignore your aids and resist downward transitions?

Is he on the forehand, heavy and pulling on the reins?

Is his tempo faster than you are comfortable with, even though it may be right for him?

Are his strides bigger and more powerful than you can comfortably sit?

Or is he running in a tempo that is faster than it should be?

A horse may run from a tight, unyielding hand. Even if your horse learns to accept unforgiving hands, you are teaching him a bad habit. You have nowhere to go, if you have 'pulled' your horse together and he is not carrying himself. You will be restricting your horse's motion; his back will be hollow and his neck short and with a short neck comes a short stride. This is a horse that rushes. It is a similar scenario to when you try to use the half halt on a horse that has no energy in his paces. It will not work. Why? Because you cannot 'check' a horse that is already laboured in his paces and heavy in the hand.

EXPERIMENT WITH THE FOLLOWING:

Have horse on the aids before the depart, self-carriage is important

Use your seat to hold him quiet and steady

Tighten your abdominal muscles

Practice lots of transitions

Ride many canter departs and always bringing him back to a walk when he starts to rush

Canter to walk, walk to canter are invaluable for helping with tempo and increase his strength

Ensure your shoulders are parallel to your horse's shoulders

Accept only a few strides of the slower tempo if your horse offers them and build gradually to longer periods

I can't really write about slowing anything without tipping a mention to the half-halt. The half-halt is the balancing aid and should be used before you ask your horse to do anything. It is very influential in making your horse obedient, balanced and 'Up' in his way of going. I have already stated that your horse must be supple and swinging through his back. The half-halt will check that swing momentarily and thus slow the tempo. Once you have mastered the half-halt, you will have all you need to slow the canter.

When I get asked 'how do you get your horse to slow down the canter?' most riders expect me to say, just do this or do that. Sorry guys. Controlling the tempo in canter is a long and diligent process and there is no 'quick-fix' button for you to install. Hence the reason it is elusive to the inexperienced rider. You have to start by assessing your horse's general way of going and build the fix(es) from there. In my view once you have mastered the ability to control the canter strides you have developed a good many skills and you are well on your way to becoming a competent rider, so worth the effort, yes?

Use of the Canter to Walk Transition

The best way to find out if your aids are correct for canter is to try walk to canter, remember to think 'Up' from a forward walk and say the word "Canter" which your horse will know from lunging. If your horse will not maintain the canter, say the words "Canter, Canter, Canter" as you ride. This is a natural progression in your horse's training. The words you have taught your horse whilst on the lunge can now be used to help you teach the ridden aids.

Often riders can achieve the walk to canter but a relaxed canter to walk eludes them; this could be a strength issue for both you and your horse and you will need patience to perfect this. Your horse needs to carry much more of his own weight on his hind legs and your weight also, during the forward transition to walk. He will find it tricky if he has not built up sufficient strength, gradually over a period of time. To help your horse develop the strength and balance to perform crisp canter-to-walk transitions, perform the exercise on a large circle. In this instance, once again, good very much begets good. You will not get a good walk unless you have a good canter. The canter should be relaxed and forward before you ask for the walk transition. If the transition is rushed, walk until you are happy with the quality of the walk, only then ask for the canter. Repeat the process, with the goal of shortening the interval between transitions. At first it might take several circles of the canter before you are ready to ask for the walk and vice-versa. It will also take several weeks of working on this exercise for a few minutes during each ride, before you will have built your horse's strength to be able to consistently canter a half circle and walk a half circle.

For you it is a matter of ensuring that you are using your abdominals and lower back to hold yourself up and keep out of your horse's way whilst he does what is asked of him in the transitions. Often riders collapse through the middle which shifts their weight and centre of balance forward, hindering your horse's ability to sit. If your horse pulls on the reins in an effort to go faster, then you should do many (and I really mean numerous) downward transitions, through trot to walk and repeatedly give and re-take the reins. This will encourage balance and rhythm on a lighter contact.

SHAPES AND ACCURACY

When meandering round the school on a long rein giving your horse a break, what sort of a shape are you making in the arena? How are you influencing where your horse is going? Are you pulling him around with the reins? Are the shapes like anything you've ever seen in a dressage test?

Essentially, even when relaxing (let us not forget your horse only does circa one hour out of twenty four in work and gets lots of breaks in that time) you should ensure that you are on a correct circle, or that when you change the rein you do it across a diagonal or in a loop, when walking around the outside track ensure you are using the corners. You should also view it as an opportunity to manoeuvre your horse around the school by the use of your seat and legs – that is without rein contact. It's all part of conditioning your horse to the movements required in a test, to listen and be in-tune with you whatever you are doing even when he is having a break. The essential message is that you should not simply slump in the saddle and allow your horse to meander; you should think about the influence you are having on your horse and use the time to do some low level work in a relaxed way.

One other point on shapes and accuracy; if you are struggling with your hands, contact, forwardness, leg position, well anything really, take a little time out to perfect your circles and shapes. Simply concentrating on having a 'round' twenty metre circle will shift your focus and before you know it those contact, hand etc., issues have dissolved. Concentrating on your accuracy and shapes can resolve a myriad of rider faults. Don't forget you will be penalised heavily by the judges if you are not accurate. It is the most basic of requirements and never the fault of your horse.

Crystal's Tip

- To aid your accuracy before your schooling session, use a rake in the arena to draw a straight line from A to C and then again from B to E, this will help you to assess whilst on board, whether your circles and shapes are accurate. It will also show you if your straight lines are straight.

WALK YOUR WAY TO SUCCESS

I like walk. I can sit beautifully (!) I can establish whatever movement I want to do in walk, I can actually do laterals properly, shoulder in, travers, half pass. And, I'm good at it. Moving up to trot and then canter can be a different matter and I remember a trainer of mine many years ago saying "any idiot can do it in walk". That's nice isn't it?

Never under-estimate the power of establishing your aids are correct and you are in balance in walk before moving up to the trot and canter exercises. It's just a matter of perfect practice to get it in the faster gaits. If you struggle, come back to walk, sort out your position, go through the movement again and give it another go. Remember, your horse must put in as much effort as you. A clean, active, forward thinking walk is a must if you are using it to strengthen your progression.

HALT, IMMOBILITY, SALUTE

The final section of this chapter about influencing your horse examines the use of the halt. If you are unable to execute a square halt, it's not down to your horse. It requires training. Make it a habit for your horse and teach him to always stand square, even for mounting, dismounting, grooming etc. If your horse is not square, have him step forward, always forward, never back to correct.

The halt is executed at the beginning and end of the test and in many tests also in the middle. Collecting easy points with a good square halt or rather ensuring that you don't lose easy points has to be a priority, doesn't it? Your entry and halt at X is your chance to make a good impression; to get the judge sitting up and taking note that someone who can ride has just entered the arena. At the lower levels it is ok to ride a progressive transition from trot to halt, the judge would prefer a few steps of walk than your horse screeching to a stop.

How do you achieve a good halt? Think of the halt as just that, a halt; a suspension of the movement; a temporary stop; a pause; your horse should be on the aids and waiting for his next instruction. If you have finished the test, you will give the rein and your horse will know it is the end; if you are starting a test, you will give the instruction to continue and your horse is primed and ready for that next instruction. He has not stopped, he has halted, temporarily. It follows then that the halt should be 'stepped into' rather than allowing him to trail out behind and amble to a stop. You need to teach your horse to halt from your seat, into a steady contact. Experiment with trying to halt your horse from walk, without your reins. You will be surprised at how effective this can be. I begin by ceasing to follow the movement of the horse and including a low 'whoa' to which my horse happily responds. This becomes a very subtle sort of 'huh' noise in a very low voice. Before I know it I have a horse that will halt from trot simply off my seat and a resisting (i.e. not following) hand.

The judge would prefer a few steps of walk than your horse screeching to a stop

It is all about being in balance at the point you wish to halt and for every second you wish to continue halting. If your legs are too far forward or too far back, you will not be in balance. Your horse will take these cues and fidget. When your legs are too far forward or too far back, may think that you are asking for the halt, but you are not. You must be still in your seat and hands, though not heavy. Your legs should hang down, neither forward of the girth, nor back, you must find the spot which says to your horse – 'halt'. It may help for you to raise your toes slightly, thereby stretching down the leg and deepening the seat. From this balanced halt you will power into your next movement. From a halt that is ambled into with hind legs trailing out, you will not.

In order to be able to positively influence your horse and thus become his trainer you need to:

Stay in balance

Have a useful contact

Which includes use of the 'inside leg to outside hand

And the half-halt

Employ the long and low frame in your training

Understand the power of transitions

Shapes and accuracy will keep you focussed at all times

Utilising the walk as a basis for all your training will keep you on track

Finally, you need to become skilled in the art of halting.

Now you might want to think about your horse's ability to carry out these exercises and help him to develop the right musculature to do so.

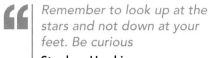

DO - Suppling your Horse

I have given you plenty to think about from defining why you ride dressage, through analysis of your body and its ability to ride dressage, to techniques to help you train your horse.

Whatever course of action you take as a result of reading The Crystal System you will inevitably go away and ride your horse. Here in Chapter 11 – Do – Suppling Your Horse, I want to examine how you can encourage and help to develop your horse's ability to execute the exercises you are asking of him. Even if you don't follow the program in its entirety you can look at a few very basic exercises that absolutely everyone can do to improve their horse's ability to bend and flex and keep him supple.

The critical aim of the preliminary training phase is looseness and by this I mean relaxation of all of the joints and muscles. Only when your horse is supple can he create impulsion, be straight and have balance with a swinging back and self-carriage. Looseness is not achieved overnight, particularly if you have started with a horse that has a degree of stiffness anywhere in his body and/or legs. It will take a minimum of six weeks of patient work for you to re-train any 'bad' muscle memory and a further six weeks for the muscle to develop and become strong.

Improve your horse's ability to bend and flex and keep him supple

Laterally your horse should be able to bend his body from poll to just behind the saddle without falling in on the shoulder or swinging out the haunches. The only means you have for acquiring lateral suppleness in your horse is lateral bending.

Longitudinally (length-wise), your horse's joints should bend and straighten equally on each side of his body with each stride; he should be able to lengthen and shorten whilst maintaining rhythm. With supple muscles comes strength. It is the act of contracting and stretching the muscles that makes them strong and supple and it is with bending and flexing exercises; lengthening and shorting of the paces that we can do this. Whatever your level of training, try to incorporate shoulder-fore, shoulder-in, travers and quarter turns into your warm up and regular training. It will be enormously valuable to you to master these lateral movements in the early stages of your training and to play a little with lengthening and shortening your horse's paces too. Just like your own stretching regime, your horse will benefit from exercises which are intended to stretch and contract the muscles, but you must do it regularly and keep it up, otherwise he will become sore.

BENDING AND TURNING

An exercise that will guarantee keeping your horse flexible and supple when regularly incorporated into your warm up is:

Walk around the edge of the arena. Ensure your horse is in a long and low frame and make an 8 to 10-meter circle at A, C, B and E.

Really feel the inside hind stepping under your horse on the circle and be sure to keep a bend through your horses whole body.

Straighten on the long sides and bend into the corners and the next circle.

Do the same on both reins.

FIGURE OF EIGHT

This exercise takes a few minutes and if you regularly introduce it into your working in, you will see a difference in everything you do, because your horse will become and remain supple. After the exercise, give your horse the buckle end of the rein and I promise he will stretch down and walk forward with purpose, because he will feel loose.

If you have ever felt, and I mean really felt what a correct change of bend feels like; flowing, rhythmic, effortless, you will know that it is worth working towards with your horse. Whilst the figure of eight exercise seems a very simple exercise, getting it right is a major building block to so many other exercises that it is really worth taking time to perfect.

A good useable rein contact
Spot on rhythm and tempo
Absolute maintenance of the bend throughout each circle
Not allowing the hindquarters to fall out
Not allowing the shoulders to fall in
No leaning in
Maintenance of the size of the circle in the correct position in the manege
Correct rising (posting) diagonal and change of diagonal
Momentary straightening through X

This seemingly simple exercise, as with all things dressage, has so many elements that can go wrong. Done properly it is not so simple.

THE TEAR DROP TURN

Of all the circles, the volte requires the most balance, engagement and power. However, changing direction through a 10-metre half-volte is something you need to master for the preliminary test. It is quite a significant movement, which should not be overlooked or thought of in any way as simple; there's more to the tear-drop turn than meets the eye.

In the teardrop turn you ride the long side of the arena, perform a half-volte toward the inside of the arena and make your way back to the wall of the long side. To ride it correctly you have to ensure your horse is straight on the long side; is supple and flexible enough to execute a half 10m circle with forwardness and rhythm and master the change of bend as you return to the track. All of this requires you to support your horse in an upright position thus ensuring there is no leaning in on the turns.

Use the teardrop turn to help you with the following:

Get increased engagement of the hind legs
Introduce counter-canter
To move your horse through changes of bend
Work on rhythm and relaxation
To help secure your connection from inside leg to outside rein
To ensure forwardness through the corners
To establish bend before asking for half-pass back to wall
Incorporate travers in the return to the track to begin work towards pirouettes.

In the return to the track, your horse has a short distance to cover and will be naturally drawn to the wall. As you progress you will use it in a more collected manner. Get the basics right in walk, trot and canter and it will be another item in your toolbox.

SHOULDER-FORE / SHOULDER-IN

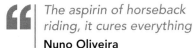

Shoulder-in was described by Nuno Oliveira as "The aspirin of horseback riding, it cures everything" and although the shoulder-in is not introduced until medium level in competition, not enough riders at grass roots levels (intro, prelim, novice, elementary) use shoulder-in and shoulder-fore as basic schooling exercises. These are essential exercises because they keep the inside hind leg stepping under and are the very foundations for helping your horse to find his rhythm and become supple. These exercises aid suppleness in your horse, make him more submissive and relaxed.

Shoulder fore is not a difficult exercise and comes easily with practice. Shoulder-in is simply maintenance of the bend that you have established for the corner all the way up the long side. I cannot stress enough, you should use shoulder-fore and shoulder-in in your warm up, every time you ride. You and your horse will feel the benefits almost immediately you begin to use the exercises regularly.

The aids: Riding shoulder-fore on the right rein, in walk come onto the long side and start as if you were going to ride a 10-metre circle in the corner. In fact you could ride a 10-metre circle and as your horse takes that first step onto the long side, half-halt and send your horse down the long side, leading with the outside shoulder. Your outside rein supports your horse's outside shoulder, the outside leg stops his quarters swinging out by coming back very slightly, the inside rein does very little but keeps the contact, while the inside leg assists with bend and activity. Aim to keep your horse regular in his rhythm, if he slows down, ride a circle or ride him forwards for a few steps then ask again. Also aim to keep your horse in balance; if he tries to rush or falls onto the forehand, half-halt or circle and start again.

I had one of my Eureka moments with the shoulder-fore. When attempting shoulder fore off the bend, approach the bend, half halt, inside leg, look where you are heading, catch the quarters with the outside leg, following seat and go. The all too familiar list of instructions that I run through when preparing for a shoulder fore, but after several attempts I was just not getting it. The conversation went something like this:

Mark	Ok, run through what you are doing
ME	As Above
Mark	Ok, but are you doing it all at the same time?
ME	Huh? – Oh, I see (Light switch ON)

So, as you approach the bend, all at once, half halt, inside leg, look where you're going, catch the quarters, following seat and allow it to happen. The milliseconds it was taking me to do these things one at a time, in sequence did not have the desired effect. All together, in the same moment, at the same time, all at once, we achieved shoulder fore.

Once perfected in the walk move onto trot and then canter shoulder-fore and once comfortable in shoulder-fore ask for more angle for shoulder-in (30 degrees for true shoulder-in). The only difference between shoulder-fore and shoulder-in is that the former is less demanding. Asking for more angle with the inside leg, makes the exercise a little harder for your horse as all the time you are asking the hind-leg to engage more with each degree of angle. This is great preparation for medium and extended work.

When riding the shoulder-in your body goes toward your own outside elbow, very delicately. It is the outside rein that is all important, try not to 'break the neck' or, put a little clearer, try not to have a break in the curved line of the neck. You should see and feel a bend from poll to croup. The secret to success is to get a few steps to begin and straighten, gradually build up to more and more steps until it is an integral part of your working regime. Ask a little, ask often and reward a lot.

When working with lateral exercises your shoulder position becomes the main focus and is of immense consequence. Essentially there is one rule. Move your shoulders so that they are always parallel to your horse's shoulders. Then, well nothing actually. Come to that you should check your shoulder angle matches your horses, on circles, straight lines and laterally. It might seem a simplistic thing to say but I have seen many riders with shoulders not matching those of your horse and your horse struggling to follow the movement.

BETWEEN SHOULDER-FORE AND QUARTERS-IN

Another exercise in walk to improve your co-ordination and supple your horse:

On a circle establish the bend

Ask for shoulder-fore on the circle, by bringing the inside leg forward a little to move the shoulder out

Capture the movement of the shoulder with the outside rein

The inside hand should be a fraction higher than the outside

Look 3 metres in front of you across the circle

It is essential that your shoulders are level with those of your horse

You are looking for a little more bend than you would normally see on the circle

Allow a quarter of the circle in shoulder fore and then release the shoulder and continue true on the circle

Next, you should ask for quarters-in by bringing the outside leg back a little

Hold everything with the outside rein

Weight into the inside seat-bone

Shoulders level with your horses

Looking 3 metres in front of you across the circle

Just a 'shift in' is sufficient, a little more bend than you would normally see on the circle

Alternate between shoulder-fore and quarters-in on the circle for about six circles, then go straight and give your horse the rein to have a good stretch. Perhaps pop into a stretchy trot to loosen and free everything up, before you go again on the other rein.

WORKING IN A LONG AND LOW FRAME

You are now aware of the benefits of working your horse in a long and low frame as discussed in the last chapter. I felt I couldn't complete a chapter on suppling without bringing in 'working in a long and low frame' again. So to refresh your memory; working in the long and low frame, relaxes your horse, balances and engages the hind quarters. Working in this frame, your horse takes long even breaths, calming him and putting him in a good frame of mind to work. Your horse's back relaxes and the strides lengthen making greater use of the legs and hind quarters. By stretching out their spine in a long and low frame, they loosen up their muscles which releases calming endorphins and helps them move in a more relaxed and elastic way. This is particularly important in the hind legs which are their 'main motor' and impulsion force. Once they are loose and working at full capacity, through a relaxed spine, your horse's movement, impulsion and expression improve. Take a look back at Chapter 10 – DO - Influencing Your Horse, to help you achieve this.

THE WARM UP

Most riders appreciate and understand the value of a worthwhile warm up. If you are to have a productive schooling session as part of the planning process you should try to establish what you need to do in your warm up to enable your horse to work at it's optimum. You are looking to remove any restrictions from your horse's body and of course, to increase oxygen delivery and blood circulation to your horse's skeletal muscles to prevent early accumulation of metabolic wastes such as lactic acid in the tissues.

But what makes a warm-up good? Is an active one better than a slow, relaxing one? How long or short should it be? Many riders with good intentions hope that a period of moving their horses around either on the lunge line or under saddle prior to their workout counts as suitable preparation. Unfortunately, this isn't always the case. In fact, a proper warm up governs the success of your training session. From a physiological standpoint, the warm up determines how much conditioning and positive physical response your horse will, or won't, receive from your training. This means that since us dressage riders (yes, that's what we are now!) are aiming to make our horses stronger, fitter, and more supple every day, our pre-workout routine could either help or hinder us.

There are many exercises you can do to warm up your horse. None of which should be too taxing, all of which should be well within your horse's capabilities and all should be done in a relaxed and forward manner. It will include walk, stretching, bending, turning circles, changing the rein, transitions, trot, canter on a long rein. Work out for yourself what the best warm up exercises are for you and your horse. Here are some suggestions for your warm up which will allow the joints to move through their full range of motion.

Five minutes walking around on a loose rein. This gentle activity allows your horse's joint fluids to begin moving and lubricating.

Once you have things moving, you can begin the warming up activity by beginning to ask your horse to stretch into a long and low contact. Spend five minutes with active forward movement in either trot or canter or both. Focus on rhythm, suppleness, and tempo on a large circle or on the outside edge of the school. Ensure it is active, with the goal of stimulating the skeletal muscles enough to force blood flow to them. Avoid the common mistake of performing suppling exercises at the start of this warm-up phase. There will not be sufficient oxygen and blood flow in the tissues to allow them pliability.

Now we can move onto suppling exercises, which may include some of the exercises above and may include school figures like circles, serpentines, and shallow loops to keep your horse listening.

Towards the end of your warm up, try some transitions within the paces to test how free your horse is feeling.

Learn to observe and feel your horse's movement at the 2-minute point in your warm-up, then the 5-minute, and at the end. Make a mental note

Does your horse feel looser?

Is he able to take longer strides?

| Is he more responsive to your aids? |
| Are there any physical signs that he is ready for work? |
| Are his muscles are warm to touch? |
| Is he salivating at the mouth? |
| Is he freely swinging over his back? |
| Is he focussed mentally? |

The above is a suggested way for you to approach your warm up. You may have other exercises that are more appropriate for you, depending on the day and how you and your horse feel. Some days I feel like my horse needs a bit of a gee up and I will have a canter round the manege in half-seat and really open her up in order to get her forward and relaxed. Other days, if I did that, I would never regain control so we stick with walking, relaxing and lateral movements to get her listening to me.

The name of the game is relaxation. This must also be your warm up goal. The important thing is not to put too much pressure on either yourself or your horse in the warm up. As you proceed, your warm up exercises should lead you directly into your planned workout for the day. This is to say that your warm up should flow seamlessly into your schooling session; you should not take a break after your warm up. Having said that Mark is a big advocate of giving his horses plenty of breaks on a long rein; short bursts of quality work, followed by total relaxation on a long rein. However, the relaxation on a long rein requires a forward and active walk, accuracy in the shapes that I perform and total attentiveness from my horse with maybe a little manoeuvring with my seat to see if she is listening.

Finally, no chapter of this book would be complete without a word about your mind-set for the training session. Don't forget to clock on as you enter the arena (don't forget you can clock off when you leave). Put every ounce of your energy and focus on your aids and your horse whilst in the arena. There's plenty of time after the session for chatter, be that with someone else or in your own head!

Empty your mind of everything other than the work you are doing; concentrate solely on what is happening in the 'here and now'.

Wow, it's all going swimmingly right? Well, no, not always, I know that and we are now going to explore a method of keeping you on track and what you can do when you feel overwhelmed (which frankly is inevitable) and perfectly normal.

We are what we repeatedly do. Excellence then, is not an act, but a habit
Aristotle

DO - Rider Focus Plan

Each small piece of progress in your training will be earned. Those breakthrough moments where, even in some small way you experience the harmony and balance that you dream of, will carry you through the times in which you struggle.

Evaluation and re-evaluation and a systematic progressive plan will ensure that the inevitable recurring plateaus can be dealt with. You may feel unable to ride, you may feel like what you are trying to achieve is just not achievable. This will continue until you become secure and master the new way of working. Often riders get to thinking 'it's like learning to ride all over again'. In the long term, the cycle of breakthrough, plateau, re-evaluation will never end, no matter how accomplished you become. However those 'bad' rides, after which you think that you will never learn to ride skilfully can and will be overcome if you continue to analyse and figure it out for yourself; no quick fix, no shortcut, no easy way - only diligent practice.

Understanding what is going wrong, thinking through the problems, finding the solutions – this is what enables progress. Any frustration and pain that arises out of mistakes are not only inevitable; they are the means by which we learn. Opportunities to be taken advantage of. The bottom line is that you should believe wholeheartedly that you can do it. Why not? Others do. The difference between Mark Bentley and my previous trainers is that Mark never compromises his standards. He demands perfect executions of the simple things. It is tedious work. It takes a long time. It takes discipline. But growth is only possible by

*Outside of your comfort zone
is where the magic happens*

stretching one's limits. By leaving one's comfort zone, that's where the magic happens. One of Mark's favourite sayings is 'What do you have when you got nothing left? – Show me what you got' – Steven Seagal. It is you that must take responsibility for the effectiveness and suppleness of your own body and the resultant affect it is having on your horse, because whatever problems you experience, sadly it is generally not the fault of your horse.

Now we are really getting down to the heart of the matter. Are you inspired? I truly hope so, if you are it's a great feeling isn't it? At last you can begin to understand the difficulties you are facing, you can stop beating yourself up about not doing it properly and do something about fixing the crux of the problem. What's more, in time, those goals you are formulating will be ticked off one by one and you'll feel on top of the world.

You will have identified your riding faults; some will have been with you forever, some will creep in and out of your riding. It seems our subconscious is somewhat more powerful than our conscious state in these matters and before you know it, those irritating faults that you worked so hard to correct are back. If you want to eliminate those faults for good, there's a sure-fire formula to success and it's not at all difficult. The solution is to make the correction a habit. We are what we repeatedly do. This is another reminder (as if you needed it) that success doesn't come overnight. When trying to correct a fault it is important to only tackle one problem at a time unless they are very small. After thirty days if you want to add something else to your routine that relates to a second issue, you can do that. You will soon see that acting without thinking, or 'automaticity' is a central component of a habit.

So, how do you install a habit? Firstly you need to select what it is you want to work on and make preparations to do everything in your power to be successful on day one. Visualise yourself being successful at what you want to do, in the car, in the office, on the yard, washing up. Emulate, as near as possible, what you want to do on your horse whilst you are off your horse. If you need to work on keeping your hands closed, when you get in the car, wrap your hands around the steering wheel and keep your fingers closed around it; if you need to smile and relax the jaw, do it constantly throughout the day (I did this one, it makes you feel great!); if you need to drop your weight into your heels, lift your toes whilst sitting at your desk to help stretch the muscles and tendons. Just be conscious of your adjustment and make it happen.

You will notice how you will revert to type simply on impulse, muscle memory perhaps. I felt completely exasperated at how very weak I appeared to be in terms of determination and my ability to keep something going; I found it more than mildly irritating how I couldn't seem to hold a thought in my head or a corrective action for more than a few minutes. But in time and with practice I have trained my brain to trigger impulses that remind me that I am trying to create a new habit, like 'you are working on your shoulders – sit up' or 'your left side is weak, use it'. Establish in your mind why the problem is happening and the effect it is having. Be absolutely crystal clear about how you are going to implement the solution.

Your issues may not be related to your body but to the way you give aids, consider why this is happening and what could be the possible causes. Then take steps to correct.

What do you have when you got nothing left? - Show me what you got

Steven Seagal

Maintain contact through bends.

Why are you dropping the contact?

What is happening at that point?

Is your horse leaning in?

Do you need to ensure you have a good inside leg to outside rein connection?

Are your hands even?

Do you have sufficient bend through your horse's body?

Are you leaning into the bend and not following your horse's movement?

Are your shoulders following the movement?

Are you looking up to where you are going with steady hands?

Are you employing sufficient inside leg?

Having identified the problem and established the root cause, set out your strategy for correcting it. There's a key difference between knowing your destination (your goal) and knowing the path you will take to get there. Once you have read this book in full you will be armed with all sorts of information that will require a plan to address your rider issues. I have called this 'The Rider Focus Plan'. You have identified your 'Big Picture', you have broken the goals down month by month until you have a to do list, now it helps to sit back armed with all the information you have and write a rider focus plan. This is the plan that you will work to in each and every session of your training. You cannot know the exact path to your goal in advance, the real purpose of the goal is simply so you remain convinced that a possible path exists. I believe that having a clear goal is far more important than having a clear plan. However in order to sort out in your mind the countless issues, a plan you must have. It will be in a constant state of flux, every day something will happen so that you have to make a change, you will need to be flexible and adapt to this ever-changing sea of activity. Remember your internal G.P.S.? Recalculate, the destination does not alter.

THE RIDER FOCUS PLAN

Area	Focus Point	Fault	Solution	Priority	Working Order	Achieved?
Training	Tempo	Too Slow	More forward movement. Do not accept slowness Lots of transitions. Get her 'hot off the leg'	1	1	✓
Position	Arms	Too much daylight between torso and arms	Feel soft arms by sides at all times	1	2	✓
Test Riding	20m Circles	Insufficient bend, not circular.	Inside leg to outside hand. Look where going. Keep everything else in peripheral.	1	3	
Test Riding	10m Circles	Unbalanced, falling in.	Not practiced enough. Incorporate at least 2 on each rein in every session. Support her with inside leg to outside rein	1	4	
Position	Lower Leg	Too far back. Too much movement	Stack head on shoulders, on torso, on hips and allow legs to dangle. Check 3-point seat. Floppy knee. Be aware of any lower back tensions.	2	5	✓
Position	Head	On right rein, tilt my head and don't look over horse	JUST DON'T! Be conscious of it at all times. Make it a habit not to. Use the mirrors.	2	6	
Position	Torso / Core	Collapsing at abdomen	Try breathing exercises. Stretch neck, prick ears, relax jaw.	2	7	
Training	Shoulder – In	Stuttery, not enough forward motion	Don't over emphasis aids, be subtle. Check shoulder alignment. May resolve with tempo issue	3	8	✓

Use the very simple table format shown to record everything you need to work on. When I went through this process I simply listed everything I could possibly think of. It ran to several pages. The secret is to put some priorities onto each one and then work out the order in which they should be addressed. The table on page 161 is a small extract from my own rider focus plan. This was a very enabling process to go through. I was utterly overwhelmed with how much work I had to do, I couldn't see the wood for the trees because I was unable to get any clarity on what was important and kept thinking about the multitude of small details I had identified. But for me the fact that my horse was not sufficiently forward came out as the number one priority and therefore, the first thing I should work on. I figured that once I had addressed this issue I could tick off at least half a dozen others because they had been resolved with addressing this fundamental problem. Likewise some difficulties are less important in terms of priority but much easier to address and so get resolved more quickly. This is just a bonus, doesn't mean you can't work on the lower priority issues, but the rider focus plan is designed to focus your mind on what is important.

RIDER FOCUS PLAN EXAMPLE

Category	Focus Points	Fault	Work on	Priority Level	Achieved?
Training	Tempo	Too Slow	• More forward movement. Do not accept slowness • Lots of transitions. Get her 'hot off the leg'	1	✓

MY FOCUS PLAN

Category	Focus Points	Fault	Work on	Priority Level	Achieved?

Getting back to making these 'bad' habits, 'good' ones, choose the habit you want to create and affirm to yourself that you will be successful on the chosen day to commence; be really positive and follow your plan no matter what. Block out any negative voices in your head and make your first session all about your number one priority and its success. Be utterly focussed; get a little obsessive; think of it as often as you possibly can.

At the end of the first successful day, celebrate. This is very important, you MUST celebrate in some small way, give yourself time to savour your success. This first day will be the cornerstone upon which you will build your overall success and will motivate you to continue in your guided efforts. You should remain focussed on this one goal. Repeat the steps you took on day one every day for 30 days until your successful way of going is beginning to form a habit.

If you don't ride every day, think about your new habit. You really do need to be a little obsessive here, it's not a problem. Remember to bring into your consciousness things that you can do 'off horse' to help and if there are things, do them.

My inability to sit straight and not distribute the weight evenly on both seat bones was the single biggest concern I had. The way it affected my poor horse was ever present. So I concentrated every ride on both seat bones and their position; I sat on a balance ball at night; I bought a posture chair for my office; I lay on the floor when I watched TV with my legs raised in order to release my Psoas; I used my left side consciously so that it was not as weak – when raking the school, when mucking out etc.; when sitting down I would automatically cross my right leg over my left, so I'd swap them over. Everything I did I some small way was contributing to my ability to sit straight on my horse and

Celebrate, in some small way, savour your success

strengthen my body. All of this is still work in progress. What is great is the fact that my crookedness is acknowledged as the root cause of many of my riding problems and I have a workable plan to help me progress in my training. Just make sure that eliminating your rider fault is your number one focus.

Here's a 10 point check list to encourage your success:

1. Commit to Thirty Days

If you can make it through the initial conditioning phase, it becomes much easier to sustain. A month is a good block of time to commit to a change since it easily fits in your calendar.

2. Make it Daily

Consistency is critical if you want to make a habit stick. If you want to start exercises, do them every day for your first thirty days. Doing them a couple of times a week will make it harder to form the habit. Activities you do once every few days are trickier to lock in as habits.

3. Stay Consistent

The more consistent your habit the easier it will be to stick. If you want to start stretching exercises, try doing them at the same time, in the same place for the full thirty days. When cues like time of day, place and circumstances are the same in each case it is easier to stick to them.

4. Get a Buddy

Find someone who will go along with you and keep you motivated if you feel like quitting.

5. Allow Imperfection

Don't expect all your attempts to change habits to be successful immediately. It took me four independent tries before I started regular stretching. Now I love it. Try your best, but expect a few bumps along the way.

Crystal Says

I need to just re-affirm that you should relish your success. If you have an off day, don't fret. Just resolve to start anew tomorrow with another cornerstone success day. You can do it.

6. Associate with Role Models

Spend more time with people who model the habits you want to mirror. Being around and watching 'good riders' is inspiring and educational.

7. Write it Down

A piece of paper with a resolution on it isn't that important. Writing that resolution is. Writing makes your ideas more clear and focuses you on your end result.

8. Know the Benefits

Familiarize yourself with the benefits of making the change. Understand the cause and effect of your bad habit. Exposing yourself to realistic information about the downsides of not making a change will give you added motivation.

9. Do it For Yourself

Don't worry about all the things you 'should' have as habits. Instead tool your habits towards your goals and the things that motivate you.

10. Keep it Simple

Don't try to completely change the way you ride in one day. It is easy to get over-motivated (!) and take on too much.

Crystal's Tip

- Create a behaviour chain. This tactic involves picking a regular part of your training and building on another 'link in the chain' by adding the new habit. For instance, instead of 'I will not look down at my horse' you could aim for 'when riding a corner the aids are … half-halt, inside leg to create the bend, outside leg to catch the quarters, weight into inside seat bone, following seat, sit up and look up'. Here you will be relying on contextual cues over will-power. You are used to thinking about the aids for a certain movement, so simply tag onto the end 'look up'. By doing this you make use of what you are already doing instead of trying to fight the current behaviours.

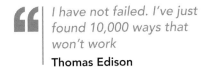

Overcoming a Crisis

The new habits you form are often very fragile, and it is for this reason that you need to eliminate any source of resistance that may lead you astray. There will be times when you think 'this is so, not worth the effort'.

In this final chapter I just want to talk briefly about what to do if and when you hit a crisis. Let me begin with an apology to those whom I may offend by using such dramatic phrasing, I do understand that not being able to bend my horse is not really a crisis. You have to put it into context. It is a crisis when it comes to your riding. Anyway, shortly after my epiphany, I hit a brick wall and seemed unable to progress in my riding. I appeared to be in an ever decreasing spiral of negativity and back in my frustrating place. I had achieved so much in such a short space of time that I was beginning to think I had reached my summit. Like some never ending treadmill, or ground-hog day - a whole bunch of clichés I know, but they best describe how I felt at that time.

When the inevitable 'curve ball' is thrown into play, you need some strategies to deal with the unexpected. Truth be told, happiness is not the absence of problems, but having the ability to deal with them. I turned to the internet to see if anyone was feeling the same out there (I do love the internet

*You need some strategies to deal
with the inevitable curve ball*

for motivational stuff). Anyway, I found what I was looking for and immediately felt better. Here's my interpretation of what I found, I hope it helps you when your curve ball comes.

REFRAME YOUR THINKING

1. Your horse is not at fault

Have you ever got angry whilst riding, jabbed your horse in the mouth, shouted at your horse, perhaps booted him in the ribs? Shame on you! Remember this, 'You are not a good enough rider to chastise your horse that way'. Whatever your horse is doing, it is because he is receiving your signals and responding to them, or because he does not understand yet what you want. It is not wilful defiance on your horse's part. If you are angry, you clearly don't understand this. If you don't yet understand this you have a long way to go. There is no place for anger in dressage.

2. Just because you are struggling doesn't mean that you are failing

I had lost my way. Whatever I tried simply did not work. I was feeling overwhelmed. Fact is every success requires some type of worthy struggle to get there. Good things take time. So I told myself 'be patient and stay positive'. Everything is going to come together; maybe not immediately, but sometime. Roll with it, instead of resisting it, in the hope that the struggle will help you grow.

3. Everything in life is temporary

Another fact, when it rains, it stops; when you hurt, you heal; after darkness there is light (you are reminded of this every morning). Nothing lasts forever. So if things are good right now, that's great, enjoy it because it won't last forever. With my riding, my things were not so good, but why should I worry? That won't last forever either. Just because you are not finding something easy at the moment, doesn't mean you can't laugh; just because something is not clicking into place, doesn't mean you can't smile.

4. Worrying and complaining changes nothing

Those who complain the most, accomplish the least. When I first read this it really hit the spot. Gosh, did I feel sorry for myself, bringing everyone around me down bemoaning my fate; spending today complaining about yesterday simply made today worse. So I decided to take action instead. It's always better to make an attempt to do something and fail than not to attempt anything at all.

5. Every little struggle is a step forward

Patience has nothing to do with waiting; patience is about keeping a good attitude while plugging away at your dreams. I decided that if I'm going to try, I will put in the time and go all the way otherwise, what is the point in starting, really? This could mean getting out of my comfort zone for a while; it could mean going it alone for a while. It was all a test of my determination, of how much I really wanted it. Guess what? The struggle is not found on the path, it IS the path.

6. Other people's negativity is not my problem.

An easy way to maintain enthusiasm and focus is to try to be positive when negativity surrounds you. Don't take things too personally, even if it seems personal. Above all, don't ever change what you believe to be right, just to impress someone who says you are not good enough. People are going to talk regardless of what you do or how well (or otherwise) you do it. If you believe strongly in something, don't be afraid to fight for it. Great strength comes from overcoming what others think is impossible.

7. The best thing I can do is to keep going.

Don't be afraid to get back up and to try again. If you are in the place where right now it seems like everything that could possibly go wrong is going wrong, like you will be stuck in a rut forever, you won't. When I felt like quitting, I reminded myself that things have to go very wrong before they can be right. Sometimes you have to go through the worst, to arrive at your best. You only have one life, this is it. Do what makes you happy and be with those people (or horses) that make you smile, most often.

8. Prioritise. Step back and take a look in.

I told you at the beginning of the book about my test pilot and how excited she became, wanting to try everything out at once. The fact is it really isn't possible to make all the changes you need to make in one go and if you try to, nothing will improve and your horse really won't appreciate it and neither will you. Take a deep breath, step back, prioritise and try not to do too much too soon.

9. Do what you do well.

I often make things too hard for myself, worse still I champion all the hard work. 'If it's important, you will find a way', 'if you're willing to pay the price, anything can be yours' in an attempt to motivate riders to achieve their dreams. When trying to overcome a crisis it occurred to me that sometimes I take too long to quit. I struggle too much; continue doing things that I don't enjoy as if working hard is what it's all about. The trouble with that way of thinking is that it implies that if you haven't yet got what you want that a) you don't want it bad enough or b) you are unwilling to pay the price. For a tiny minority, this may be true. I say may be true. There may be some people out there who are simply too lazy, too dispassionate, too uninspired to take action to get what they want, but I think that they are the rare few. Many just don't have sufficient clarity about what they want.

When I had my 'crisis' and everything appeared to be going wrong, I went back to the very beginning and asked myself the question 'why am I doing this?' The reality is that I already worked too hard, too long, putting forward too much effort and it was the very effort that I put into things that was costing me results. You see, excessive effort makes things too tense and too serious and eventually it all goes a little sour. That's not to say that effort or work is a bad thing, it is excessive effort and work that is, I believe, a perfect recipe for finding unhappiness. After asking myself 'why am I doing this?' I went back to doing what was well within my capabilities and did that for a while; stopped pushing myself; re-established the basics; stepped back and took a little time out. I needed it; we all do from time to time.

EMOTIONAL INTELLIGENCE

The New Zealand All-Blacks Rugby squad are considered to be the toughest, smartest, and most successful sports team on the planet. With an impressive 86% success rate you'd expect them to train hard, have a robust team culture and be tactically brilliant. What you might not expect is that they spend a lot of time and energy working on their emotional skills, an area which most of us totally ignore.

The All-Blacks treat emotion as muscles to be trained. So when players were having trouble controlling their emotions in competition it was recognised that they were trying too hard and it was all to do with their emotional state. They needed help. Interestingly navy pilots refer to this as OBE: 'Overcome By Events.' I have to tell you I was somewhat relieved to discover that the same emotional turmoil, centred on my sport, had not only been recognised but systematically worked through by the All-Blacks and Navy Pilots. Well, you can see I am in good company.

Have you ever heard of the phrase 'Emotional Intelligence'? It is the ability to identify, assess and control our emotions, to use the information we gather about our emotions to guide our thinking and behaviour. Control of your emotions will depend on how much you feed them, that is, how much focus you give them. Control requires us to understand them, recognise when and why we feel this way and have the tools in place to influence them.

Think of any stress or anxiety you are experiencing as a 'thing'. Not some mystical happening that can't be dealt with. Turn it into an object, visualise, if you like – a little monster. This little monster – 'spiralling anxiety' can blind us into thinking that now is all that matters. It makes us rush around, snapping and barking, it's hungry and has a way of making us feed it. At stressful times look ahead beyond what is happening now. You'll see the big picture you've created. It'll feel better. The first step to emotional control is to know when we are actually being emotional and why. You can't control your emotions by ignoring them. If you feel stressed acknowledge that you feel stressed –"Okay, I don't like this, I'm feeling very stressed!" Now you've admitted it to yourself.

Next, identify why you feel this stress: "This is because I'm late to the yard, having driven for hours in horrendous traffic and I feel robbed of my quality time with my horse". Why you are feeling it means you're that much closer to doing something about it. The tendency is to think that moods just happen. They don't. There has to be a very particular set of circumstances in order for the stress to build and influence our behaviour. Remember I spoke about your basic human needs and scoffed because I felt that someone purchasing a dressage self-help book would not have the need for food and water met? Well there is an element we can take from this in dealing with stressful situations and the inability to think straight and that is hydration and hunger. If at times of high stress, like the period after work when the days 'shizzle' hasn't been dealt with and you are on your way to the yard, if you have skipped lunch or not had a drink for four hours, it will be harder to suppress the anxious feelings. We can influence, even change, our moods without resorting to alcohol … Ahem! Learning how to do this is a very powerful tool. So, try these three small exercises to turn your stress around:

1. **Instantly do something else.** Just do or think something different. Don't be passively carried along, allowing the stress to consume your thoughts.   So, I'm driving along wishing I was at the yard an hour ago, I'm hacked off! I take a moment to strongly imagine feeling relaxed and comfortable and even in a good mood. I consider what it would feel like to have all the time in the world – this will, at the very least, neutralise the bad mood.

2. **Breathing. Here it is again.** I love breathing, it's so useful! You already know how important correct breathing is in your riding; now give it a go to help you cope. You need to deal with the physical changes, as always, led by the way we breathe. Anxiety can only 'work' if we are breathing quicker with shallow breaths. Reset your breath by holding it for 5 seconds. Breathe in slowly, focussing on your diaphragm. Breathe out even more slowly (imagine that you blowing calm into your hands (on the steering wheel if you are driving). Remember, it is the OUT breath that creates the calm, let it out a little longer than the IN breath.

3. **Force the thinking part of your brain to wor**k. This will dilute and subdue the rampaging emotional part. Having recognised that the little monster 'stress' is making an appearance, force yourself to remember three names of riders that you admire and why, or the names of horses you like and why, or even just run through the alphabet in your head. Try it, because it really will work.

CRYSTALLIZED AND FLUID INTELLIGENCE

As an aside, I named this system 'The Crystal System' before I became aware of the Cattell-Horn theory of Fluid and Crystallized Intelligence. This theory suggests our intelligence is composed of a number of different abilities that interact and work together to produce our overall general intelligence. Whilst 'Fluid Intelligence' is the ability to think and reason logically, i.e. the problem solving bit, 'Crystallized Intelligence' involves knowledge that comes from learning, based upon facts and rooted in experiences. It is said that as we age and accumulate new knowledge and understanding our Crystallized Intelligence becomes stronger. I took some comfort from this, knowing that my capacity to learn can only improve with age, you should too. This theory sits well with my thirst for knowledge and understanding, and coming across the term 'Crystallized Intelligence' in my research was a bit of a gift, one of those messages which says 'yes, you are on the right track'.

GET EXCITED AND GO - COMPETITION NERVES

There will come a time when you are ready for your competition. You may already be competing and doing well, but for those of you that often face competition demons, here are some strategies to help. Your fears may not relate to competition but other aspects of your riding. Have a read through as this advice has resonated with many, many riders who do not compete.

Anyone who has experienced competition nerves will know just how devastating they can be. Someone swapped your horse for one that is so much more sensitive, hot and strangely problematic. For your horse it's a case of 'who is this person riding me and what have you done with my mum?' (Or dad or usual rider). But please have faith. With time, patience and a grand plan (sound familiar?) you will be able to control your nerves and ride at your very best. But you need to work on it, like everything else that needs training you must look at this problem as a training issue, for you, something to be incorporated into your 'Rider Focus Plan' and worked on alongside all your other training topics.

The thing that is at odds with this situation is that nervousness is the body's way signalling potential dangers and protecting us from doing anything rash. All very well if we are in a dangerous situation, but at a dressage competition, really? When you put it into context you can begin use the anxiety you are experiencing in a positive way. Let's have a look at what is happening to you.

Your body is releasing adrenaline. The rate at which it releases affects your body's reaction to it. Symptoms can range from anxiety, doubt and negative thoughts, through to nausea, sweating, dry mouth, migraines, an increase in breathing and heart rate, even diarrhoea. If this all sounds depressingly familiar, the good news is that nerves can actually aid our riding; speeding up our reactions and making us ride with more purpose. But, the bad news is, for some they make the whole competition process one humungous emotional trial. For those of you in the latter group, you need to learn to work with your emotional responses. But firstly you will need to understand them.

Perhaps you have had a previously bad experience. Pin point for yourself exactly why you are feeling these 'nerves' and ask yourself what would be the worst possible outcome?

Are you concerned for your personal safety?

Is it that you fear you will not be able to deliver a competent performance in front of others?

Or is it something else?

Perhaps a reality check is in order.

How many times did something negative happen at a competition venue and you didn't die?

How many times did you get asked to leave a venue because your riding was so bad?

How many times when you thought you rode badly did you NOT get asked to leave a venue?

How many times did you witness a crowd of people standing pointing and laughing at your lack of ability?

How many times did your friends walk away, refusing to acknowledge that they know you as a result of your riding?

Do you see where I am coming from? If you are nervous because you think everyone is watching. Remember, though people are more concerned with how they are doing than with watching you. Even the spectators are more concerned with who they are there to watch than with how your test is doing. The next thing to do is to establish precisely what is happening to you.

Are you creating pictures of everything that might go wrong?

Are you playing out a running commentary of negativity in your head?

Are you creating a drama that doesn't exist?

Are you making excuses for failing before you have even tried?

Your body will not differentiate between what is real and what is imagined. What you are thinking and feeling is reflected throughout your body. Think about replacing the word nervous with 'excitement'. You will be amazed at how your brain will adapt and generate a totally different state.

The very best way to help your brain relax and not feel the need to press the alarm bell is to try to keep your body soft and relaxed; you will find it hard to generate anxiety from a relaxed body. How? Here it is again, the superb art of breathing. Learn to ride with slow breathing based low, behind your belly button. If you get really good, you can synchronise your slow breathing to your horse's strides in any pace, this will help you maintain your breathing and a good rhythm. Really practice this as part of your training at home so that it becomes second nature to you at the competition. Holding your breath unconsciously will cause tension and you could even become light headed. When you concentrate on your breathing your jaw will relax. If not, open your mouth very slightly and keep your jaw 'floppy', by doing so you are telling your brain you are relaxed and it will react accordingly. Also try smiling through your test. Smiling can help you to feel more positive and it looks good to the judges.

Use your peripheral vision. Something else you can only do when relaxed and therefore you can trick the body into thinking you are relaxed by putting yourself into a soft, blurry gaze where your eyes remain firmly fixed on one spot in front of you whilst taking in everything around you by way of vague shapes, colours and movement. Learning to ride like this makes it difficult for your brain to generate a negative state because it is not natural. It will also improve your balance and sense of feel and again you should master this at home before the competition.

Why not have a caller for your test if it's allowed, certainly until you get over the problem. A word of caution; don't use this as a substitute for learning the test in advance. Not knowing your test will exacerbate the nervous condition. Having a confident and calm friend there will help boost your confidence and keep you focussed. Stay away from nervous people. Both are contagious.

Focus on your test, each movement individually and how you are riding. Do not rush. There's no hurry to finish. If your self-talk is all "this is horrible, I can't do this, my horse is going to run out of the arena, I can't sit the trot, I don't belong here, I am useless, I can't ride, what on earth happened to my horse?" simply banish it. It is emotional baggage and needs offloading. Why would you put your energies into this and not learn to stay rooted in the moment, concentrating on what is actually happening underneath you, right now? Being more positive will decrease the adrenaline secreted in your body and will help with breathing. It is important to explore what the most helpful thoughts are for you individually before you ever get to the show.

I CAN DO THIS:

I'm so proud we got here

How beautiful is my horse?

We are developing a really good partnership

We have come a long way together

I am so privileged to be doing this

I love my hobby

Let's show the judge what we can do

The tool the All-Blacks use to control their emotional state is called 'Red Head/ Blue Head'. Red Head is the negative state; heated, overwhelmed, and tense. Blue Head is the cool, controlled state, when you deliver top performance. The tool encourages you to devise personal triggers to make the transition from Red Head to Blue Head in the competition environment.

Try to remember a time when you were on your horse and felt the best you have ever felt. Attach a word to that memory and bring yourself back to that feeling through the repetition of the associated word(s). This will re-affirm that you have done it well before and you can do it well again. It will put you in 'Blue Head' mode. So I use the words "Clint Eastwood" whenever I feel tense. For me it is a memory of one canter in a warm up at a local competition, when I just felt like it all came together. Even now as I write, I am smiling and I feel a very warm, satisfied feeling – it really was good though! … and I am feeling this because I said 'Clint Eastwood' and remembered the feeling of that canter. Clint would have made a good dressage rider, so relaxed and 'at one' with a horse.

MORE HOMEWORK BEFORE A TEST ...

Take a few minutes three times per day to mentally rehearse yourself riding confidently.

Be extra prepared before the test, know all the movements of your tests by heart and how you are going to ride them.

Be sure that all your equipment, tack and horse are ready before the show so you have less to worry about.

Be on time and know the way to the show venue (in case you have to leave in a hurry! Hahaha)

Do some physical exercise that morning or the night before to reduce anxiety.

Have a hot bath or shower before you leave for the show to help relax you.

Don't eat too heavily before you go. It will sit in your stomach like a rock and make you feel worse. Have something light and nutritious and bring some healthy snacks with you.

Stay hydrated. Plenty of water will keep the anxiety monster at bay.

Repeatedly watch your favourite rider in person or on video. Recently neuroscientists have discovered 'mirror' neurons in the brain that activate when you watch someone do something that you are actively learning about. Very interesting stuff. The idea that I can ride like Spencer Wilton just by watching him is pretty exciting, don't you think?

Take on board Charlotte Dujardin's philosophy – "I always look at it as the same old centreline, just another arena," Or as she more directly and more famously said, "same old shit, different arena."

Remember, confidence is like a muscle, the more we use it, the stronger it gets. I have a little story for you to illustrate the power of mind over matter. One time, whilst out hacking with Mark who was riding my sorely missed old boy Archie, (a typical thoroughbred), with me riding another horse, we heard the roar of a motor-cross bike on the track ahead, but because of a sharp bend we were unable to see it.

More to the point, it was not going to see us. Soon enough, a couple of youths appeared riding the bike, hell for leather and screeched to a halt a few yards away from us. Mark was so incensed that he turned Archie towards the bike, kicked him on, cantered straight up to the youths and with the horse peering over the handlebars of the revving bike, gave them a piece of his mind. That done, he turned and trotted back to me, I was aghast! Not because of the incident but because Mr "I will spook at my own shadow" Archie Boy appeared completely un-phased by the whole thing. You see, it's a simple state of mind. Your horse will reflect whatever your state of mind is. If you are confident, so will he be, if you are thinking he will spook, so he will.

MAKE FAILURE YOUR FRIEND

Most people seem to have an innate fear of failure. I started this book by saying "What isn't ok is the way it made me feel about myself; essentially an epic fail". This was not a good place to be, but with hindsight failure actually became my friend. It was the catalyst that I needed to go out and find a better way. People who succeed also fail a great deal because they make a lot of attempts. There is nothing wrong or shameful in failing. The only regret lies in never making the attempt. So don't be afraid to experiment. Sometimes the quickest way to find out if something will work is to jump right in and do it. You can always make adjustments along the way.

There is no final destination, dressage is a lifetime of learning

Understand that failure is not the opposite of success. Failure is an essential part of success. Once you succeed, no one will remember your failures anyway. But if the word 'failure' is currently an abomination to you, then reframe it; you succeed or you have a learning experience.

You will by now know that I am a huge advocate of planning I have stated that dressage is a 'thinking sport', 'it's all about the strategy' but as with all things dressage you have to apply balance. Some people can get bogged down in planning and thinking and never get to the point of doing. Try not to get stuck in the state of analysis paralysis. Letting go of the fear of failure will serve you well. If you're excited about achieving a particular goal, but you're afraid you might not be able to pull it off, jump on and do it anyway. Even if you fail in your attempt, you'll learn something valuable and can make a better attempt next time. When in doubt, act as if it were impossible to fail because in essence, it is. Remember, everything in life is temporary.

I firmly believe that your first step is to know exactly what you want. You must know your destination with as much clarity as it is possible to achieve. Make your goals S.M.A.R.T. and put them in writing. If you cannot define your destination precisely, how will you know when you've arrived? When you have achieved a goal, take a little time to enjoy the satisfaction of having done so. Absorb the implications of the achievement you've made towards other goals, make any adjustments to your goals and focus plan and move on to the next. When reviewing the rest of your plans think about these things:

How easily did you achieve this goal? Make your next goal harder.

Did the goal take a dispiriting length of time to achieve? Make the next goal a little easier.

Did you learn something that will lead you to change your other goals? Then do so.

Did you notice a skill deficit, despite achieving the goal? Decide how you are going to fix this. Perhaps an additional goal.

If you don't already set goals, start now. Try this technique as part of your everyday life, you'll find not only your riding but other areas of your lifestyle accelerating and you'll wonder how you ever coped without it.

MY FINAL THOUGHTS …

We all have doubtful moments when we think …

Why does it all have to be so intense?

Why am I so hyper-critical?

Why does it seem that nothing is ever quite right?

Why can't I just have fun?

These questions will crop up from time to time. All I can say is that it is fun, but it is serious fun. When you get it, you will feel like you've never had so much fun. I feel passionately that even if you do not agree with the entire Crystal System method, you will find something in this book to help you on your dressage journey. But, just in case you missed the thread that runs through everything I believe, I want to leave you with a final thought. Keep things simple. Simplicity is the key to brilliance. When I say simple I realise that this can be misunderstood, it doesn't necessarily mean 'less' it means 'reduce to its heart'.

When you reduce what you do to its very essence you couldn't take anything more away without it becoming ineffective. Likewise, anything you would add is unnecessary and would only really create clutter and confusion. Usually everything we aspire to do goes through an evolution; a cycle of development until the process comes to rest at the 'essential state'. This is where it nears perfection for its purpose. When you try and learn something new there is usually some seemingly chaotic input. It's hard to separate the relevant or even essential elements from the irrelevant but as you learn more you start to set the pieces of the puzzle together for yourself. In time, you arrive at the mastery stage, where you just know. The process can become very intuitive and once you become aware of it you can sense if something is essential or not.

If you apply this principle to something as straightforward as applying your leg aid, it can be beautifully demonstrated. Remember how relieved I was to discover that I didn't need immense strength in my legs for them to be effective and the 'less is more' lesson that I learnt. The nagging and bumping with the leg became counter-productive. In this example, the use of the leg aid is stripped back to its heart. Give your aids, then half the applied pressure and see if you still get the required result, if the answer is yes, half again until you strip the aid back to its essential state where in time you will 'think' trot, your body will automatically react by doing the absolute minimum required and you will lift effortlessly into the transition.

Similarly, in the example where I was training my horse to halt I began by including a low 'whoa' to which she happily responded. This became a very subtle sort of 'huh' noise in a very low voice. Before I knew it I have a horse that will halt from trot simply off my seat and a resisting (i.e. not following) hand. Each element of the aids is reduced to its heart; reduced to its essential state. No more. No less.

It all comes down to your ability to be clear about your goals and how you are going to get there; your ability to question, evaluate, re-evaluate and apply. Put all your endeavours into developing the ability to see the straight to the heart of what you are trying to achieve and only do what is needed to get there. When you are confronted with a new situation ask yourself: "What is at the heart of this? And "How does this fit into what I already know and what I already do?" Is it essential?"

I highly recommend that what you do next is to go back to the beginning and re-read this book now that you have an insight into the whole system, because each time you do, you'll notice something new. As you progress through your training, different elements of the book will resonate with you. As you revise and refocus; the book will act as a reference manual throughout your journey.

Knowledge is not power, crystal clarity is where the empowerment comes from
Patricia Pitt 2014

I wish you the very best in everything that you do. Allow the light of The Crystal System to help you shine.